Understanding and Working with Difficult People
Revised Second Edition

Joseph E. Koob II

Revised Second Edition

All rights reserved. No part of this book may be used or reproduced in any manner whatsoever without written permission from the publisher. Printed in the United States of America.

Second Revised Edition, 2019.
Copyright © 2006 by Joseph E. Koob II

For more information visit http://www.difficultpeople.org

A difficultpeople.org publication

ISBN: 9781696740623

Books by Dr. Koob

Business Trilogy: Dealing with Change

Difficult Situations - Dealing with Change

Honoring Work and Life: 99 Words for Leaders to Live By

Leaders Managing Change

Business Trilogy: Succeeding at Work

Dealing with Difficult Coworkers

Succeeding with Difficult Bosses

Managing Difficult Employees

Dealing with Difficult Customers

Caring for Difficult Patients:

A Guide for Nursing Professionals

Books with a Personal Focus

Understanding and Working with Difficult People

ME! A Difficult Person?

Dealing with Difficult Strangers

Difficult Spouses? Improving and Saving Your Relationship with Your Significant Other

Succeeding with Difficult Professors (and Tough Courses)

Guiding Children

A Perfect Day: Guide for a Better Life

Writer's Digest Merit Award

Best book Non-fiction Oklahoma Writers Federation

Preface

This book is designed to be a practical, accessible introduction to the very broad topic of dealing with difficult people and difficult behaviors. Since every difficult situation is different, the focus here will be on building a basic understanding of how you interact with difficult people, what makes difficult people tick, and the most fundamental skills you can bring to the table to help change these encounters for the better.

On difficult people

Who is a difficult person?

What characteristics or what behaviors qualify a person as difficult?

We will cover these topics in some depth during this book. First, however, I would like to suggest that the label, "difficult person" unfortunately has a negative connotation and feel to it. When you think about the difficult people in your life – that negative connotation may be appropriate. You may even use considerably stronger terminology for identifying the difficult people in your life than this, e.g. idiot, jerk, ogre... and so on.

One truth, however, is that we are all negative at times. Labels always narrow our perspective and understanding. Perhaps a better term for a difficult person would be "socially challenged" or "the occasionally socially challenged." It does seem silly, though.

The best way to be successful with someone who you feel is difficult is to focus on the behaviors that are creating this angst between you. We can be successful dealing with a behavior; it is much harder to be successful with a difficult person.

I hope that this book will provide you with the information you need to begin to reclaim your independence and life from 'difficult people'. Our goal at difficultpeople.org is to provide the most comprehensive materials and support available for helping you be successful with concerns you have with others. We have many books available that provide an in-depth perspective for working through difficult people concerns. This book is the foundation. See Appendix IV for an annotated bibliography of other titles available or visit our web-site at www.difficultpeople.org for a comprehensive listing of all the materials and services we provide. Many of our books are also available at major on-line retailers.

Thanks

Generally, a thank you section is reserved for all of those supportive people who have helped to make this happen. However, I would first like to thank all of those difficult people who have shown up in my life, because they have gotten me to this point. I would especially like to thank the REALLY DIFFICULT people (this would be a good place for one of those other terms) who have inspired me to make this study and the difficultpeople.org site a reality.

Special Thanks to

Special thanks to Heath Potter, my long-time webmaster and creative design specialist who helped put this web site on the map.

My lovely wife, who probably has to put up with some occasional difficultness on my part.

My son, Nathan, and also my good friend, Anne Duston, who both helped with the drafts; and my daughter Elise who always inspires me, just because.

Terri Voight, VP of difficultpeople.org and coach extraordinaire, for her encouragement and input.

And to all of those friends who have given support and encouragement. You know who you are.

Thanks!

Chapter 1

Key Ideas

Introduction

There are many books about coping, dealing, and working with difficult people. All of them have important ideas and fundamental truths that can help us deal with difficult people more successfully. They also all have a certain bent or emphasis, based on the author's experience and background. After making an extensive study of the difficult people literature, my hope is that I have been able to draw these ideas into a comprehensive whole that will provide you with a broad conception of what you need to know to understand difficult people; and to ultimately cope, deal, work, and be successful with them. I imagine this book will also have my own personal orientation from my experiences as a mentor, coach, counselor, manager/leader, and as a well-intentioned human being in dealing with the difficult people that have crossed my path.

By keeping the orientation of this book general, I hope this will allow you to gain a knowledge that will apply to a far-reaching spectrum of difficult situations. You will then have the foundation upon which to build your knowledge and skills through further reading and study in more specific areas relating to difficult people. [See Appendix IV for an Annotated Bibliography of our books and the Bibliography for an extensive listing of difficult people materials.]

This introduction presents what I feel are some of the most important concepts you will need to know to be successful in difficult people situations. You will see these ideas interspersed throughout the book. Keeping these key concepts in mind will help you keep the many ideas throughout the book in focus.

Through the course of writing many books about "Understanding and Working with Difficult People," I developed a short list of Key Ideas I felt are the most helpful in being successful with difficult others and in difficult situations. An annotated version of these *Seven Keys to Understanding and Working with Difficult People*, are presented in Chapter 13 I encourage you to read these several times and refer back to them frequently as they can serve as a foundation for your work and success.

The Seven Keys
to Understanding and Working with Difficult People

Self-Awareness

Self-worth

Self-confidence

Self-control

Honesty

Kindness

Positivity

A Difficult person?

After contemplating many descriptors for a difficult person, I decided that the most fundamental, broadest perspective is best –

A Difficult Person: Anyone who causes anyone else angst.*

*Irritation, upset, stress, anguish, anxiety, perturbation

Which, when you think about it, means **all of us**

Which in turn leads to another truth about 'difficult people' –

If you think of another person as being difficult,

it is highly likely that they see you as being difficult

The point we ultimately want to focus on is **"what are the behaviors they exhibit that cause us angst."** When we can focus on their behaviors, we have a far better chance of succeeding with them, than if we are trying to succeed with a 'difficult person.'

There are as many <u>types</u> of difficult people

as there are difficult people.

Reading through the literature you will find many attempts to delineate specific categories of difficult people by assigning labels like: Tank (Bully), Thumper, Exploder, Snake, Bossy, Grudge, Ape, etc. While these are very useful toward focusing our attention on what drives these 'types,' it is the <u>behavior</u> of these difficult people that affects us; and labels, no matter how useful, tend to narrow our thinking. Toward the end of this book we will discuss behaviors that tend to be found in many 'difficult' people and the skills you can bring to bear to help deal with these behaviors.

By focusing on behaviors, we can begin to understand what motivates a person's difficulty. This understanding then allows us to develop and direct specific strategies and skills for being successful with them.

Another important consideration in being successful with a difficult person is that a given 'type' of difficult person, e.g. a Bully, typically exhibits behaviors of other types, the Sniper, Grudge, etc. They also will often change their behavior to another form of difficult behavior if they run into someone who will not accept their bullying. In other words, they try to get what they want through other, less than ideal, behaviors. By focusing on the specific behaviors they use, you CAN make a difference over time, and this person will eventually learn that you are not willing to accept whatever technique they are currently using to manipulate you.

You can only change yourself; you cannot change other people...

We should add the word **directly** to the end of that sentence:

"You cannot change other people directly, however..."

Often,

when you change your own behavior,

it causes the difficult person to change his/her behavior.

Difficult people, like all of us, have regular patterns of behavior. We use these patterns because they get us what we want. If we, as the victim, move from **reacting** (we surrender our control) to **responding** (we gain control of ourselves, and often the situation), the difficult person will NOT get what they wanted and may change their behavior toward us as a result.

Most difficult people do not know they are being difficult.

Think about this one for a minute, because if we feel we have to deal with a REALLY difficult person on a regular basis, it is difficult to comprehend that they don't have a clue about how they come across to others. This statement is true even when **most** people see them as hard to get along with.

From my own experience, many people who exhibit difficult behaviors are oblivious to the pain and frustration they perpetrate on a daily basis. I truly believe that some of the most aggravating personalities I have met have no idea how they are affecting or coming across to other people. In fact, typically they see themselves in an entirely different light.

> Author's Note: I sometimes work for clients who want me to help out with a difficult person situation. Even when the person is

aware that other people find them difficult, they have a very hard time understanding why. It is often about how we look at the world and ourselves.

Finding out what the difficult person wants, needs or cares about is KEY to understanding and working successfully with them.

The better you understand what is important to the person/people you are dealing with, the easier your task will be to move from being a victim to being in control of your own destiny with that difficult person.

The difficult person is getting a reward for his/her behavior.

We all do things for a reason. It feels good or it helps us feel less bad. When we do things for others, we do it because we want to help others and because it feels good to help others.

Difficult people are using learned behaviors because the behaviors have worked for them in the past to help fulfill a need, want, or desire. However strange that might seem to us, they are getting something from their difficult interactions with others.

It is actually quite common for all of us to use a variety of behaviors that we found useful as children, in our regular interactions with others. 'Difficult' people tend to use behaviors that most of us have decided are inappropriate for use as adults, e.g. whining, blaming, temper-tantrums, etc.

Negativity breeds Negativity

Positivity breeds Positivity

This is such an important key to working with difficult people that I had trouble deciding which part of this to put first. Throughout this book we will be emphasizing a positive, in-control, self-confident approach to difficult people. The more you can remain calm, cool, and collected the better. It is amazing how your **positivity** can help defuse even the most difficult situations.

Another way I like to think of this is,

Negativity never helps.

It just does not. Think about it!

Unfortunately, most of us have found negativity useful in the sense of 'getting us what we want.' The truth is that we can always accomplish the same thing by remaining positive, and we will do much less damage to sensitive egos when we can. It takes a good bit of **self-awareness work**; as well as maintaining our own positivity through thick and thin, to consistently do this, though.

[Okay, I admit it, I like to make up my own words sometimes, but it seems like if we have **negativity,** we ought to have **positivity.**]

You can learn a tremendous amount from difficult people.

As a long-time educator I always look at the world from the perspective of "What can I learn from this?"

Here is a teaser:

One thing I can always learn from difficult people

is

how NOT to be difficult.

People are different

This is the most common cause of difficulties between people!

When we are willing to bring to the table a compassion for the differences in people, we are miles ahead of the game in dealing with a person who is causing us upset. Prejudice, bias, and narrow-mindedness are the cause of too much pain and suffering in the world, and are far too often at the root of problems with difficult people. You can afford to be magnanimous, because you are **self-aware** and **in-control.** [See Chapter 13, *The Seven Keys to Understanding and Working with Difficult People.*]

Make an effort to understand that they have as much right to be here as you have; and that whatever is driving their difficult behavior, it is something that at that moment in time they probably don't have much control over (as much as you would wish that they would). Your self-control and your kindness may lead to a fundamental understanding on their part of a better way to behave. If not, at least you have risen to the occasion as a human being who cares.

Kindfrontation is so much better than confrontation.

Sandra Crowe, in her wonderful book, *Since Strangling Isn't An Option: Dealing with Difficult people–Common Problems and Uncommon Solutions,* uses the term "carefrontation" as a way of approaching difficult people, instead of con(against)frontation.

I LOVE this idea. However, I tend to think along the lines of kindness when I interact with people, so with a respectful nod and thanks to Sandra, I'm going to use "kindfrontation" in this book.

This leads me to a little gem from Wayne Dyer (see Bibliography),

When you have a choice between being right and being kind,

choose being kind.

This is such a simple, beautiful idea; but at times, particularly times when we are besieged by a difficult person, it is very hard to do. If you can give up your claim to being right, you may be surprised at how much of your anger, fear, frustration, and pain just wash away.

Honesty IS the only choice

Tempered with kindness, honesty is the only way you can successfully work with difficult people. Anything short of this is asking for more trouble. Yes, sometimes it is difficult being completely honest, but it does pay, BIG TIME!

There are always ways to be honest AND kind when communicating with others.

Questions/ideas for contemplation

Try writing one or more of the key concepts found in this chapter on a piece of paper and place it in your purse or wallet. Dig it out and read it again and again throughout your day. You will be reinforcing some very important ideas, and I am willing to bet they change your day for the better. This is especially effective when working with the *Seven Keys to Understanding and Working with Difficult People* on a regular basis.

Go to www.difficultpeople.org to find our current contact information.

PART I

Me, Myself, and I

Chapter 2

It is all about Attitude: YOURS!

You may be surprised to find that a major part of this book is about YOU. That is because it is what YOU bring to the equation that makes all the difference in working successfully with difficult people. In the next few chapters you will learn just how critical your attitude, approach, self-control, and focus are to helping you in difficult situations.

But...

What about **their** ATTITUDE?

You are right, of course. In difficult situations we tend to focus on the other person's attitude. When someone else is being rude, boorish, negative, over-powering, whiney, etc., it is very easy to pay more attention to their behavior and more difficult for us to turn that around and focus on our behavior.

If you can turn your attention back to yourself for just enough time to PAY ATTENTION to how you are feeling, what you are thinking, and how you are about to react, you can be successful in many, perhaps even most, difficult situations, and quite possibly with some really difficult people. [See below, *Catch It, Check it, Change it*, and Chapter 8, *Reaction or Response*]

Paying Attention

These two words became a highlighted item in my book, *A Perfect Day: Guide for a Better Life*, and I didn't realize how important it was until I had written the whole book and was rereading it.

When we pay attention to ourselves, we gain something essential in our dealings with other people, and absolutely critical when dealing with difficult people – we gain control – self-control.

Who is in control?

Most difficult people are trying to get control. It is one of the most common characteristics of a difficult personality. Unfortunately, with their tactics, whatever they may be, they often achieve exactly what they want.

7

They have learned to push other people's buttons as a means of controlling them and the situation

Wanting to be in control is also a general characteristic of the human race. None of us likes to feel we are not in control, or to feel we are being controlled by others. It is the amount of control we try to wield over others that makes the difference between someone we and others may see as difficult and, well, hopefully the rest of us.

We will discuss the difficult people side of control more in a later chapter. For now, we want to focus on YOU and what you can do to make a difference.

Being in control

The object of paying attention to yourself is not to control others, but to be in control of yourself. At the root, this means not giving over your emotions, your power, your behavior (reaction) to another person. It has to do with **Self control** and **Assertiveness**.

Assertiveness is, fundamentally, being able to stand up for yourself in a positive way.

Assertiveness will be the focus of the next Chapter.

Staying in control of you

Several years ago, when I was working at the VA Medical Center in San Diego, I was fortunate to work with Dr. John McQuaid. In the course of my writing several manuals for drug and alcohol group therapy, John introduced me to something he had written for use with the patients. As with many good ideas this one is simple and easy to remember:

Catch It

Check It

Change It

While the concept isn't new, the **3 C's** makes it easy to remember.

Catch it!

The first step in gaining and maintaining self-control in a difficult situation is to **Catch** yourself. Paying Attention equals "Catch it"

By paying attention to your emotions, what you are thinking, and the reaction you are about to have, you set yourself up for making a choice.

Choices...

...are everything in difficult situations. Rather than buying into the other person's mania or difficulty and immediately reacting, you can now be who you want to be – who you **choose** to be. You make the choices.

Check it

While this may seem like the obvious next step, it is not always so clear cut. You want everything about this difficult situation you find yourself in to be very clear for you. Checking it helps you set up making different choices than you would normally make.

Take a look at your feelings, your thoughts, and your soon to be reaction. Is this really how you want to feel, think, and react?

The bomb didn't go off?

The simple act of checking these inner workings of your mind and body does a very important thing. It sets up a pause in the 'proceedings.' That pause means you are still in control and you haven't let your emotions take over. It will also, very likely, puzzle the heck out of the difficult people. He wants and is waiting for, the expected reaction from you – loss of control – anger, upset, frustration, fear, etc.

Change it

Then you have the choice of redirecting yourself and the situation. As you will find out, this makes all the difference in the world in dealing with difficult people.

Remember

> **Catch it** – are you paying attention to yourself?
>
> **Check it** – is this really how you want to be?
>
> **Change it** – make a different choice

While it is important to pay attention to yourself, it is important to pay attention to the person you are dealing with, too. The first part of this book is about what you are bringing into a difficult situation; the second and third parts of this book focus on understanding what the other person is bringing to the equation.

Questions/ideas for contemplation

What kind of attitude DO you want to bring to a difficult situation?

Think of difficult situations you have been in recently and imagine taking these extra moments to stay in control. Can you see yourself making other choices?

Try practicing **Catch it, Check it, Change it** in a variety of situations this week. They don't have to be difficult situations. Just see if you can get the hang of it. You might be surprised at how much control you suddenly have – control of yourself and the choices you make.

Chapter 3

Being Assertive

How we present ourselves to others

Aggressively?

Passively?

Passive-Aggressively?

Assertively?

We probably all have moments where we fit into each of these three personality types. We may use a wide range of approaches to others throughout our daily lives. For example, sometimes it can be helpful to be a bit more aggressive in certain circumstances when working with others (hopefully with understanding, kindness and compassion thrown in). Or we might find a passive approach useful at other times. However, when dealing with a difficult personality, your best approach is being assertive.

It is probably better to think of these as characteristic ways we approach different situations. People who are seen as difficult by others tend to use non-assertive (aggressive, passive-aggressive, passive) approaches, as their regular means of attempting to control situations and other people. When this is how they typically approach interacting with others, it can be very frustrating to those who have to deal with them on a regular basis.

We will look at each of these types very briefly in this chapter. Then we will discuss them at some length when we focus on difficult personalities in Part II of this book

Aggressive behaviors

You know aggression when you see it. Aggressive people push the rest of us aside in their fervor to get what they want and to maintain power and control. Aggressive personalities want, try, and need to control others. This usually goes beyond what we or others are comfortable with and goes past what we should be willing to allow. No one has the right to bully you. No one has the right to try to control who you are.

Food for thought: Are aggressive people the most difficult to deal with?

Passive behaviors

Passive people tend to let the world flow around and over them. Their best mode of defense is to stay out of the way. It is also how they are able to maintain control of their world. They can be frustrating simply because we

11

can't seem to get anything out of them. They may be perfectly happy not
being involved and have no desire to have their comfortable, out-of-the-
mainstream existence disrupted by a more aggressive type.

Passive-aggressive behaviors

Passive-aggressive personalities can be the most damaging of all. While
they will usually come across to others as passive, accepting, "yes" people,
they often can be quite aggressive behind people's backs. They like to
maintain control far from the lime-light where and when they think you are
not paying attention. They are able to get their way through manipulation,
innuendo, lying and cheating, back-stabbing, etc.

Assertive

Assertive People stand up for themselves with quiet self-confidence.

They know their human boundaries.

(Brinkman and Kirschner)

Assertive people have control over themselves, not others. They maintain
their integrity in the face of even the most difficult situations with difficult
people.

Betty Perkins in her book, *Lion Taming*, states,

"To 'be in integrity' is to be how you want to be in all settings."

What a great perspective, not only on assertiveness, but on life.

Sandra Crowe also has a unique perspective,

"Passive people wait to be told, aggressive people tell,

assertive people ask."

(Since Strangling isn't an Option)

By learning to be assertive in the face of aggression, passivity, or
passive-aggression, you can set a far different stage for success. Coupled
with **understanding, kindness,** and **compassion,** being assertive allows
you to stand up for yourself without the situation escalating. The ideas,
skills, and techniques found throughout this book presume you will
approach others from an in-control, self-confident stance – you will be
assertive despite how they present themselves.

Being Assertive

> "Determine in your heart to sing your own song." (Meier)

Assertiveness can be very difficult when we are facing a tirade or even when trying to work with someone who just isn't responding. To re-emphasize, the key to being more "in integrity," to being more assertive, is to pay attention to yourself and then to make adjustments when you are feeling overwhelmed.

By watching who you are in a given situation you are stepping back and giving yourself the power to respond – in a calm, in-control, self-confident manner, rather than just reacting defensively without clearly making a choice.

Catching yourself in the act

When I consciously started on my personal road to self-improvement some years ago, one of the first things I latched on to was watching myself in different situations. I could literally be in a difficult person situation and watch myself react to the difficult person as he/she pushed my buttons. At that time, I wasn't maintaining much control over my reactions, but I was watching.

That simple process, which does take practice, is the first step in moving from a victim position (from which you might react aggressively, passive-aggressively, or passively), to choosing a self-confident, success-oriented approach. It is the first step in becoming assertive.

Flunked assertiveness training?

So did I for far too many years of my life. Learning to be self-confident and to maintain your self-control takes practice – lots of practice, if you are not already there.

> Note: There are many materials and approaches to assertiveness training. Covering this in detail is far beyond what we are trying to present in this book. However, if you feel you could benefit from such a course of action, go for it. You will learn a great deal and you will be in a far better position to deal with difficult people successfully. Try searching the web for Assertiveness or Assertiveness Training or search on-line book retailers with these keywords.

You can also practice **paying attention** to yourself and to others; as well as applying and practicing the **Three C's: Catching yourself, Checking yourself, Changing yourself** in given situations. These self-awareness practices will help build your self-worth, self-confidence, and self-control* in difficult circumstances, which will help you become more assertive in your dealings with others.

***Self-awareness, Self-worth, Self-confidence**, and **Self-control** are four of *The Seven Keys to Understanding and Working with Difficult People.*

Be patient

Self-change does take time. While it may seem simple to say, "Don't react; stay calm; be yourself," when we are in a situation where everything inside us screams to react and defend ourselves, it is very difficult to do. It can take a while to move from, "Hey look I'm getting angry here," to actually being able to NOT get angry, and to move from a **reaction** to an **in-control response** to a difficult person's attacks. Keep working at it!

Questions/ideas for contemplation

Try watching how you approach different situations. Which type of approach are you using – aggressive, passive-aggressive, passive, or assertive? If you are not completely in a confident, self-control mode, can you move yourself in that direction?

Something to think about:

> When we are **defensive** (blaming, whining, critical, giving excuses, etc.), we are not in an assertive mode. We often become aggressive, passive, or passive-aggressive.

Chapter 4

Emotions

When someone else's behavior frustrates us, our emotions are involved. We may get angry, feel embarrassed, feel down for awhile, and so on. The better we can understand how our emotions and how our reactions impact the situation, the better.

Emotions are not bad – they are our way of telling ourselves that something is important in our life at this moment in time. It is how we deal with and understand our emotions that makes a difference. When we can move from allowing our emotions to take over, to a position where we can choose what happens next; we can maintain **self-control** and typically maintain control of the situation. This has a great deal to do with **self-awareness** and **self-worth**. [See The *Seven Keys to Understanding and Working with Difficult People*, Chapter 13]

He makes me very angry!

He is angry. He is being loud, over-powering, rude, and may be downright scary in his behavior, but he is NOT making you anything. As bad as his behavior gets, you have a choice in how you react.

What he is probably doing is pushing your buttons. He is REALLY good at pushing buttons. It makes him feel in control. It may even help him feel superior to others. It is his way of maintaining his very fragile ego.

NOTE: I indiscriminately use gender throughout the text. No specific emphasis is meant, i.e. men and women can be equally difficult.

What are you feeling?

The first things we bring to bear when we encounter difficult behaviors are our emotions. We react to what another person is saying or doing because it touches something inside ourselves that seems to require a reaction. **Paying attention to how you are feeling as a difficult situation develops is key to being able to control yourself and ultimately the situation.**

Egos

Whenever ANY negative emotions are present, in us or in them (difficult people), **egos are at work.** Our egos seek to maintain, at the very least, a balance of power, control, and a sense of self in any situation in which we feel threatened personally.

One of the primary characteristics of people who are consistently negative and difficult is a **poor self-image**. They maintain their personal equilibrium by using less-than-ideal tactics to feel in control and powerful. Unfortunately, this almost always affects others in ways that make them feel put-down, abused, angry, etc.

When we react negatively to negativity from another person, we move from our self-worth into ego. **When we can manage our emotional reactions by responding in a calm and in-control manner, we stay within our own self-worth.**

Our Hot Buttons

Some difficult people seem to enjoy finding and pushing our buttons (our emotionally sensitive areas); others just roll right over us without considering how we are feeling. Because of their behavior, we find ourselves feeling things that we don't really want to feel: frustration, anger, shame, guilt, and so on.

Sensitivity to certain types of behaviors in others can be a natural reaction to an outside stimulus, e.g. if someone attacks us, we want to defend ourselves. Being sensitive can also have something to do with things that bother us from the past.

In either case, we can react very strongly.

For example:

> If I was consistently put down by an important person in my life as a child (mother, father, teacher, etc.), I will very likely react strongly to any derogatory behavior from another person that says, in effect, "You are not good enough!"

What this emotional reaction tells us is that our self-worth is taking a hit. As we work with our self-awareness and as a direct result, our self-worth and self-confidence, we learn to move away from these types of reactions to more in-control responses. As we build our self-worth, we are able to be less and less affected emotionally by these types of negative behaviors from others. It does take time and effort.

It is **how** we respond that is critical.

Flight or Fight

Generally, there are two primary reactions to difficult situations: we want to flee or we want to defend ourselves (maybe both). One really key idea about working with difficult people is that neither of these choices works very well. We will talk a good bit about other choices, other responses you can make, when we discuss understanding difficult people and their difficult behaviors.

The past infringing on the present

Some of our most intense fight or flight feelings come from deep within us as a **re**-reaction to hurts we have suffered in the past. It is far beyond the scope of this book to delve into a long discussion on past wrongs and the reactions you may have as a result. YOU are the person who can best understand why and how you react to negativity in others through careful self-observation. However, it IS important for you to realize that these triggers can exist. **By watching your reactions to a difficult person, you can learn a great deal about what is bothering you inside.** This gives you the opportunity to acknowledge and work on those past ills if you wish.

Learning about our <u>self</u> (who we are and what we are bring to the table), and focusing on our emotions, gives us greater self-control and self-confidence. As we build our self-worth, behaviors that used to set-off our hot buttons, no longer bother us as much as they used to. Eventually, we can reach a stage where these old triggers don't bother us anymore when someone tries to push them. Their stuff; not ours!

The result?

> We feel better about ourselves.

> We no longer feel bad because of other people's insensitivity – that is their stuff and we don't have a need to buy into it anymore.

> We change our reactions to their behavior and hence, they no longer get a reward for their negative actions. With no reward, the behavior typically changes toward us.

Acknowledge your emotions

By watching your feelings in a difficult situation, you are doing two important things: you are stopping yourself, even if it is just for an instant, from just reacting; and you are also giving yourself the opportunity to acknowledge what you are feeling. [See Chapter 1, *Catch it, Check it, Change it*, and Chapter 8, *Reaction versus Response*]

This is a very important skill to learn toward your developing self-control and in being able to deal with these intense feelings.

As you continue to practice self-awareness in difficult situations, you will able to take a step back in my mind and watch what is boiling up inside. You might say to yourself, "I'm really getting angry, here." "I'm getting upset." "My stress levels are rising." And so on. Just this personal acknowledgment can help to defuse some of the tension and angst. And knowing how you are feeling in response to someone else's negativity allows you to start to make other, more positive choices, for yourself.

That is the first step toward building your self-worth, self-confidence, and self-control! You still feel your emotions, and it IS important to feel and acknowledge your emotions, However, you have also set the stage for making a choice as to how you will respond. Choices and options help you maintain control!

IMPORTANT!

Stuffing your emotions is NOT a good idea. They will just come back to haunt you in the future.

Sometimes we manifest our stuffed emotions in difficult behaviors toward someone else, e.g. taking our anger out on another person (colleague, spouse, family member). Facing your emotions and understanding them is a much better choice.

What do I look for?

Try to put your emotions into words – it helps them become more concrete.

An excellent technique and habit to get into is to write down how you are feeling, or felt, when you are reacting to some stressor. For example: if your boss, a volatile type, comes in and yells at you about something and then leaves, take a brief opportunity to write a paragraph or two about how you are feeling. This gives you a solid foundation from which to build your self-understanding. Plus, the act of writing down what you feel helps you to deal with and get in-control of your emotions.

If the situation precludes your being able to sit down and write something out, do it later. It will still be very useful and it will help you understand and work through your typical emotional reactions to someone else's negativity.

Sometimes it is hard to put your finger on exactly what is happening. The next time you are feeling an intense negative emotion in reaction to another person, try 'being with' the emotion and focusing on what you are feeling (and thinking – we will talk about working with our 'thoughts' in Chapter 6), and what is happening in your body.

Bodily sensations

We respond to our emotions physiologically. When you pay attention to your body when feelings arise in an encounter with a difficult people, you will be able to actually describe what is happening: "My chest is tightening," "I'm starting to sweat," etc.

Watching the physical sensations, you are manifesting during an intense emotion gives you the chance to be an independent observer. In a sense, you can stand back and observe all that is happening in your body and see how all of this is affecting you. It is another step toward understanding yourself and being able to control your reactions, while still experiencing what you really are feeling.

What happens next?

Emotions are important indicators of what is going on inside ourselves. The important idea here is that you can learn a great deal about yourself by paying attention to your emotions. You are able to acknowledge them; and then as a result, you have the choice to react or respond in new ways.

Once you have checked in with your emotions, you can take the next step, which is to ask yourself the very important question:

> "Why am I feeling this way?"

Or you can phrase it in any number of other ways:

> "Why is what this person is doing bothering me so much?"

> "What about this person's behavior is setting me off?"

This helps you begin the **process of self-understanding**. When you recognize the triggers to your intense negative emotions, you have set the stage for understanding what sets you off and why. The more you develop this process, the more you will understand yourself. Eventually, you will find that these triggers have less and less effect.

It is important to realize that everything that irritates us about other people can lead us to a better understanding of ourselves. (Crowe)

You will have learned a very, very important lesson – an emotional lesson – which is:

> **No one can make you FEEL anything**

"He makes me very angry," revisited.

The whole discussion above is about understanding that you **choose to feel a certain way**. If you take a moment and imagine a difficult person you have in your life and their really difficult behavior, you will probably feel emotions starting to well up inside you. It may not feel like you really have a choice except to react strongly to them. However, as we learn self-control, as we develop our self-confidence, and as we begin a process of self-discovery through our new practice of self-observation, we find that we do have other choices.

Important point: the more we do this, the more we practice, the more choices we have.

> **Are you going to let difficult people MAKE you feel anything?**

Questions/ideas for contemplation

You can practice observing your emotions and potential reactions by sitting quietly and imagining being with a very difficult person. Then go through the process described above. You will be ahead of the game the next time you encounter this person, or someone like them.

What are your hot buttons?

Try making a list of the different types of behaviors that trigger your most intense emotions and reactions. Then try to think about what the exact opposite of each "button" is.

> For example: if someone putting you down (a typical difficult people behavior) is a trigger for you, then the opposite would be someone "putting you up," or praising you, supporting you, etc.

A good starting point for this exercise would be:

> "I get really upset when...."

and then counter that with,

> "I would feel much better if...."

For example:

> "I get really upset when someone lies to me, or talks behind my back about me."

> "I would feel much better if people could be up front and honest with me all the time."

These are great exercises to help get you started toward succeeding with difficult people. They help you delineate in writing behaviors that cause you inner turmoil and give you a clear picture of how you would like to be treated by other people.

Practice saying the positive statements you develop to yourself during and after encounters with someone who pushes your buttons. Positivity breeds Positivity!

Chapter 5

Emotions II

Difficult people make me...

Remember: difficult people don't MAKE you feel anything!!! It is your choice to respond to them in a certain way. You can ***REACT!* OR** you can **choose to respond** (and stay in control of your emotions).

Difficult people often provoke a wide range of negative feelings, that is why we call them ***DIFFICULT***. Really difficult people can trigger the following emotions and reactions and many more:

Anger	Sadness
Hurt	Frustration
Hate	Guilt
Shame	Stress
Depression	Sense of loss
Fear	Emptiness
Worry	Loneliness
Anxiety	And many more

Filling in the blank, "Difficult people make me...." can tell you a great deal about what emotions you are typically bringing into a difficult people situation.

A better way to phrase this to eliminate the concept of someone being able to 'make' you anything is to say to yourself,

> "When X gets angry with me, I feel________"

Or,

> "When Y treats me badly, I feel________"

This is another good exercise to practice writing out. Keep writing about your feelings and how you typically react. Try to get everything associated with this behavior down on paper. Write until you have nothing further to say, then leave it for awhile and come back to it again later.

21

For example:

> "When X gets angry with me, I feel really angry. My temper
> flares and all I want to do is fight back even though I know it will
> just make things worse. I also feel hurt. I don't understand why he
> does this or what I have done to deserve this. It is so frustrating, I
> want to scream. Then when he leaves, I start winding down and
> begin to feel guilty. I…"

Guilt is a very common emotional reaction to negativity. We wonder what
we have done to cause someone to treat us this way. As in the above
example, guilt may not be your immediate reaction. However, if you did
this exercise and worked through it for several minutes you might realize
after writing several other feelings you have toward X's anger (anger, hurt,
stress) you may find this one buried. That is why it is helpful to continue to
write until you feel you have said everything you can; then to come back to
it later, re-read what you have written. Add to it if you recognize other
elements to your reactions.

Understanding how we react to another's negativity helps us learn a great
deal about who we are and what is important to us. It gives us the personal
power to make changes, too.

Love and Fear

> "There are only two emotions – love and fear –
>
> and you are perpetually feeding either one of them."

Betty Perkins states this in her wonderful work, *Lion Taming: The
Courage to Deal with Difficult People Including Yourself.* After I read this,
I pondered it for some time and realized that there was a good bit of
wisdom in this statement. Since then, I have found this same idea
expressed in several other, non-difficult people literature, sources.

This is an interesting and thought-provoking perspective on emotions.
Take a moment to really think about what this means. What does it mean
to you when you consider the many ramifications of thinking of all positive
emotions as founded in love, and all negative emotions founded in fear.
This is heavy stuff when you think about it!

Fear: the centerpiece for negative emotions

Take another look at the negative emotions listed above. When you really
think about it, they do all seem to be motivated by some 'fear factor.'

If you think about the two most common reactions to difficult people and
difficult situations, flight or fight, you can see the connection more easily.

Sadness, hurt, guilt, worry, shame, loss, etc. all have to do with 'flight' or avoidance, and anger, frustration, hate, etc. have to do with 'fight.' Generally speaking, they all have to do with defending ourselves in some way.

Anger

Anger (rage, frustration, getting mad) is probably the most common and one of the most intense feelings we can have during interactions with difficult people. It really does feel like that whatever they have done – yelled at us, put us down, blamed us, etc. – is making us angry. We tend to get very defensive (and sometimes very offensive in our defense).

However, if you look closely at your angry feelings and sensations, you will probably see that they are rooted in fear. The more we understand our fear, the easier it becomes for us to deal with anger and other negative emotions. Try looking at your negative feelings closely the next time they arise in a difficult situation. See if you can recognize everything that is driving this feeling that is welling up inside you.

Ask yourself:

What am I afraid of?

You might be surprised at how powerful that little question will become in changing your whole life for the better. Fear thrives on the unknown. When we begin to understand and know ourselves, a good bit of fear can dissipate from our reactions to difficulties.

Negativity never helps

It just does not! I used this phrase in my book, *A Perfect Day: Guide for A Better Life* (1998). And it is well worth repeating.

Negativity NEVER helps

The more you can take this to heart, the more positive your days will be – even difficult people days.

Love – the centerpiece for positive emotions

Love is a tough term for some people to relate to as it brings up a whole realm of relational ideas and concepts. If the word love is a bit too much to swallow, try substituting 'kindness' or 'caring.'

Kindness – the centerpiece for positive emotions

Or

Caring – the centerpiece for positive emotions

Think of a list of positive emotions, for example:

Happiness

Joy

Love (in all it is varieties)

Elation

Ease

Gladness

Warmth

Well-being

Abundance

And so on.

These all have to do with feeling good, and isn't love the ultimate good feeling?

Negativity versus Positivity: it is your choice

> Which would you rather choose?

> An easy choice, right?

Then why do we waste so much time feeling anxious, frustrated, worried, angry, and so on?

You do have a choice! And now that you can step back and watch your emotions and acknowledge those emotions, you can begin to make wiser choices.

Two beakers

I often use a story as an imagery tool when I give motivational speeches.

With this little story, I set the stage by talking about coming across a most wondrous, clear, beautiful pond of water in a clearing in the woods. It is so beautiful that we immediately dive in and become one with the pond. We discover very quickly that there is one basic tenet for life in this pond:

> Every time anyone has any type of negative emotion or thought
> (even worrying counts!), we add one drop of gunky, yucky,
> sludgy water to the pond of life; and every time we have a
> positive, kind emotion or thought, we add a drop of crystal pure
> water to the pond.

What are you adding to the pond of life?

A good exercise is to keep this in mind for a few days or a week and imagine collecting your drops of yucky, sludgy, gunky water in one beaker and your drops of crystal-clear water in another. See how full your beakers are at the end of each day (or week). For the next week see if you can make some improvements and lower the gunky, yucky, sludgy water level and raise the pure water level.

Taste buds

Which beaker would you be willing to drink at the end of a week?

Mix the two beakers together. Are you willing to drink the water now?

Working on our positivity really takes work. But it is well worth it, because how you bring yourself emotionally (your **attitude/mood**) into a difficult situation can make all the difference in the world. **The more positive an attitude you can bring to the situation, and the more you can maintain that, the more likely you will be successful.**

Remember?

A key concept is,

Negativity breeds Negativity

Positivity breeds Positivity.

Practice positivity...

      because it works,

      because you will feel better,

      because all the people around you will feel better, too!

And...

A positive approach is sometimes all that is needed to defuse a difficult situation or to 'change' a difficult person. (Osborne) It can change how they interact with you, which is probably one of your main goals in understanding and working with difficult people.

A final word

A realistic goal in working with your own emotions and how you interact emotionally with difficult people is to,

"Stretch your comfort zone so that you can stand comfortably

in the presence of your own

and other's fear and its manifestations."

(Perkins)

It is no small task, but it reaps huge benefits and it moves you further along the path of being successful with difficult people.

Questions/ideas for contemplation

Make a list of negative emotions you feel when you are in a difficult person situation. Can you see how these feelings are motivated by a fear factor within yourself? Or is there another, more global emotion you could link these under?

Make a list of positive emotions **you would like to feel** when you are in a difficult person situation. How would you describe these emotions using an all-inclusive term?

Work toward the one you really want to feel.

Chapter 6

Thoughts

Which came first?

Remember the chicken and the egg? When you are in a difficult situation, for example, say your boss just steam-rolled over your elegant proposal, which comes first?

> Your thoughts about how he/she is acting and what he/she is saying?
>
> or
>
> Your emotions?

This could be a hard call to make because both seem to kick in fairly fast in difficult situations. Our tendency is to react first (our emotions) and contemplate later, even if this sequence happens in quick succession. The important consideration here, however, is that we need to develop the skills to examine and acknowledge both our thoughts and emotions.

Catch it

As a difficult situation unfolds, it is very useful to look at our thoughts and how they impact our emotions. By taking that very quick pause and making an effort to step back in your mind during an encounter and observe your feelings (see Chapters 4 and 5, *Emotions I and II*), **you can stay on top of what is happening mentally**. This can help you delineate the things that are bothering you about another person's behavior and your reaction to it. The better you understand the situation and how it impacts you, the more **self-control** and personal power you will develop.

When we react emotionally in a difficult situation and follow that up with negative thinking, we can drive our emotions further in an unwanted direction. The concerns and stress can escalate.

Instead…

We can make an effort to **Catch** our negative thought process, examine it (**Check it**), and try to turn our typical reaction around (**Change it**). This can be a very helpful process in defusing your negative feelings and potential negative reaction(s), and has the potential to defuse the whole situation. [See also Chapter II for an introduction to this technique.]

Checking it

The first thing you want to check is whether your thoughts are based in or around any negative emotions (as discussed in the previous two chapters). **When you are aware of your thought process, you can gain control of your emotional reaction and begin to direct your response.** In other words, you can control your reaction (emotions, thoughts, and actions) to this difficult person's negative behavior and impact, and in many cases begin to control a more positive direction to the interaction.

What are you bringing to the table?

We are going to ask another very important question later on in this book,

What is the difficult person bringing to the table?

Because understanding what is motivating them and how and what they are doing is also key to being successful with them. For now, we want to focus on what you understand about yourself and your reactions; and what you can do to make a difference. Personal power in difficult situations starts with you!

Understanding both of these perspectives will enable you to be much more successful with difficult people. We will talk a bit more about perspectives and attitudes in the next chapter.

What you bring to the table are your,

> Emotions

> Thoughts

> Words and Actions

When you can maintain control and avoid negativity, you have set an entirely different stage than if you lose control and react. As you work with the skills and techniques in this book, you will learn to have the control and power to not only respond differently, but to add positivity to the mix.

Positivity breeds Positivity

Be patient – some really difficult people take a long time to come around. Your quest is to make a positive difference for YOU. If you also help make a positive difference for them, then you have really made a difference with your life.

Prejudice, Bias, Preconceptions

The first word of these three terms conjures up all types of negative associations. It is not unusual for prejudice and bias to be a significant factor in difficult person situations – especially if we are dealing with a real doozy of a difficult person.

However, we all have our little biases. We all bring preconceptions to our interactions with others. These can seem to be very, very little things. You may not like: perfectionists, overweight or skinny people, people who smoke, left-handed people, people who eat noisily, people who don't work as hard as you, people with dimples, people who find it hard to make decisions, people who sit with their legs crossed..."

Some of these seem really silly, but they are all things that can influence our perceptions of another person right from the start. We all make these instantaneous little judgments. Knowing how these can influence our interactions with others is a key to being successful in difficult situations.

Knowing what your small biases are, can help you pull them out of the situation with a difficult person and allow you to look at the whole person and not their 'stuff.' You can learn this by examining your thoughts (**Catching, Checking**) when you think about a person that you often have trouble coping with. Do this over the course of several months and you will find that you regularly make judgments of other people based on your likes and dislikes, some of which may have nothing to do with who the other person really is. [See Chapter 14 on *Differences*]

A good exercise to try is to watch your thoughts, **your little judgments** of people on a day to day basis – everyone you run into. It is amazing how often a judgment just slips in there as soon as we see another person:

> "She is too...,"

> "He certainly has...,"

> "I wonder what she is doing with..."

Judgments and biases are not necessarily all bad. These types of thought processes can be negative, neutral, or positive. The real trick is to begin to shift our negative preconceptions toward more neutral and positive thoughts. Next time you have a quick negative judgment of another person, counter it with something positive about the person. Begin to train yourself to see the good in others.

Even the worst difficult people have redeeming qualities. When we focus on and reinforce the good, they are much more likely to try to bring those to the fore in their interactions with you.

Preconceptions

Your preconceptions about a difficult person can add a great deal of fuel to the fire, especially if you have had negative encounters with this person before. Acknowledging that you have built up a reservoir of 'stuff' about another person can help you step back and take a longer, deeper look at what you bring into any interaction with that person in the future.

Can you shelve that stuff and give this difficult person a new start?

The truth is that unless you are willing to make the effort, even if they 'started it,' the situation is not going to get any easier for you. Sometimes we have to swallow a little pride and give up our need to 'be right' in order to have peace and equanimity in our lives. Make positive choices for yourself and for others – **in spite of their behavior!**

Changing it

The first step in changing our (pre)perceptions of anyone is to acknowledge that we have them. I have some. I have never met anyone who didn't. We all bring 'stuff' to the table in our interactions with others. Acknowledgment gives us a chance to change or neutralize our stuff about another person.

The second step, is to examine it. This can include trying to understand what use this conception has for us. Is it adding to the negativity of the interaction or is it something that can add positively to the relationship?

If it is not adding to the relationship, your interactions with this person, then you need to work toward changing it. Try to move at the very least to a neutral position or thought, and at best try to redirect it toward a positive position or thought.

Once you are in control of the thoughts, having 'caught' them and checked them, this is not as difficult as it may sound. In many ways the first two steps aid greatly in neutralizing a preconception or negative feeling about another that comes up in our interactions with them.

Controlling your feelings and thoughts

The last three chapters have been about NOT letting others, and what they do, control your feelings and thoughts. You now have the tools to begin to reverse that process and take control of your own thoughts and feelings.

Remember: you can only control yourself and that really can give you an amazing amount of power in any relationship. Learning to use that power wisely and kindly can create a whole different world for you in your dealings with others.

Questions/ideas for contemplation

What types of preconceptions, small biases do you bring to a difficult person scenario?

A very powerful exercise: take some time to write this exercise out in detail. You will probably be very surprised at how much you can get out and reflect on in a short period of time. This self-knowledge will give you a powerful stage to build from in working with the difficult people in your life

> Think of the difficult people in your life and then write down all the negative thoughts you can generate about them.

> Can you think of ways to turn some of these around, to neutralize them, or even have a more positive outlook for the next time you encounter them? Write these down as well.

For a jump on a future chapter:

> What preconceptions about <u>you</u> is your difficult person bringing to the table?

Thinking about this can help you understand what is helping drive their behavior toward you.

Chapter 7

How you come across to others

When I am with my difficult person, I really feel....

How would you fill in the blank? How would you fill in the blank again and again with a different answer each time?

> When I am with my difficult person, I really feel...stressed.
>
> When I am with my difficult person, I really feel...depressed.
>
> When I am with my difficult person, I really feel...nauseous.

This exercise focuses on your feelings and in any difficult situation your feelings play a huge role. They affect who we are and what we do in the situation AND they are almost always recognizable to the other people involved, even when we try to stuff or hide them. By **paying attention to your feelings** (this exercise helps you make that knowledge more concrete), **you can begin to understand how another person may see you**.

> **Difficult people often take advantage of our feelings.**
>
> **It is part of their power and control games.**

This section continues the discussion of the three previous chapters with a bit broader look at how we approach a situation with a difficult person.

Mood

> Can you describe your feelings when you think about a difficult person in your life?
>
> Can you identify your overall mood?
>
> Considering all you have learned so far, can you envision yourself bringing a more positive approach into your next interaction with a difficult person?

Take some time to answer all of these questions. You will receive some valuable insight about yourself, and you will have taken another step toward self-understanding and toward ultimately being successful with difficult people in general.

The focus is on YOU!

What you bring into a difficult person situation is more important than what the other person brings to the situation.

This is a very important truth **because YOU are the person who can make a difference!** When you have the self-control to bring a more positive <u>you</u> into the mix, the situation is already a hundred times better than it was before.

Upset, anxious, tense, uptight!

You very likely had a specific difficult person in mind when you decided to read this book or you might have had a generic type of difficult person in mind. The last thing you feel is calm, cool, collected, and positive. When you think about them, it is probably hard to imagine being positive with this...this...person.

They are people, too

To start with, yes, they are a person. They have as much right to be here on earth as the rest of us. They have their faults, their needs, desires, loves, dislikes and so on. They may be vastly different from us and those differences may bother us a great deal; however, understanding and working through the differences we have with others is one of the ways we can become a kinder, more compassionate person in difficult situations…

Even if they are 'at fault,'

Even if they started this whole thing,

Even if they are completely rude, boorish, and obnoxious

YOU are the only person who has the personal power, control, and compassion to turn this relationship around – OR – you could continue to deal with it as you always have, but that probably hasn't been much fun. Try to think of the following, as often as possible, throughout your day:

If you are not having fun, something is wrong – adjust.

(Koob)

Adjust in positive ways. You will be glad you did. And everyone you interact with will be glad, too.

Compassion is about...

Compassion is about recognizing them as a whole person. Getting past:

Their faults

Their attitude

Their foibles

It is about:

Being kind

Caring about their humanity

Being in the spirit of what being human is all about.

Respect other people, not because they are wrong,

or even because they are right,

but because they are human.

(A slightly rewritten thought from John Cogley)

At times, perhaps far too often, we lose sight of the important fact that there is something very fundamental that we all share. When we really think about it, even when we try hard to put our fingers on what it really is, it is never easy to describe. What makes us human? What is our humanity?

But when we do make that effort, we take a step higher on the ladder of what humanity is all about.

Compassion is kindness in the most difficult of circumstances.

(Koob)

How can you get there?

This is the first big step toward approaching your difficult person more positively. It is basic and simple, but not always the easiest thing to do when they are being really difficult:

You just have to remember they are human, too.

The next steps we have already discussed: **pay attention** to your thoughts and emotions as they arise (**Catch them**); examine them (**Check them**); and then work toward **Changing them.**

The work

This positive work can be a task, a challenge, or even fun. It is all in how you approach it.

One key is to **plan ahead.** Go through the steps above over and over as you think about, feel, what it will be like to be with this person again. Then imagine yourself responding in a different way – stay as calm as possible within your mind and body and decide HOW you want to come across to them.

This might help

Think about or imagine how you would like them to come across to you in a similar situation.

Then BE that person. Put on that positive 'suit' or persona and see how it fits. It may feel a bit strange and awkward at first, but keep trying it on for size. **It is much more fun being positive. It is a choice you can make.**

When you practice this type of work in your head several times, it helps set the stage for you when you next encounter this person. It will help your confidence and your ability to follow through with a new approach. Remember, you have to stay within your own **positivity**, your own **self-worth** and **self-confidence** in spite of how they react or what they do and say. Work through the entire scene in your head again and again. It may not play out this way in reality, so be prepared to be flexible and to make on the spot adjustments.

The absolutely, positively most important, key idea

You do have a choice!

You **can** control your feelings, thoughts, mood, and attitude.

Author's Note: I used to teach a college entry course for freshman entitled, *The Student Success Course*. The first day I would be a boisterous, happy, easy-going professor. At the end of that first lecture, I would ask them to write down the main things they hoped to get from the class and then have them turn in their lists.

At the beginning of the second class meeting, I would storm into the room, slam my books down on the desk, and proceed to tell them how lousy and ridiculous their responses had been. I would rant and rave for several minutes. You could see the absolute shock in their faces – some almost got up and left. Smiling faces would suddenly change to frowns, mouths dropped open, shoulders slumped. The whole atmosphere of the class, lively and easy going before I stormed in, changed in a few moments as they reacted to my negativity and anger.

I stopped in mid-rant, sat down on the edge of the desk, and smiled. Then I told them calmly and positively that **attitude** was the most important factor in their doing well in college. They got the point.

It IS all about how we approach things. **Our attitude IS that important!**

Questions/ideas for contemplation

How do you think your difficult people would react to a complete change in attitude on your part?

One of the truths of human kind is that we tend to stick with our programmed ways of interacting with people – **change takes effort**. Think of some ways you could change your approach. This will be a good lead-in to the next main section on dealing with difficult people.

Chapter 8

Reaction or Response

Do you **react** negatively to the difficult people in your life?

There is a better choice.

We <u>react</u> in stressful situations

Not to worry, it is natural. Animals have instincts. We humans have some as well.

Have you heard the term 'knee-jerk' reaction? That refers, I'm assuming, to when an M.D. hits us on the knee with that little hammer. I have always thought there was some purpose for that little maneuver by doctors. Maybe it was to coin this phrase.

If you think about it, we all have knee-jerk reactions. One very common knee-jerk reaction is how we react to a physical attack. If a person starts to swing at you, more than likely you will duck, throw up an arm to block, or back away. It is instinctive. If you have ever taken Karate or Taekwondo, your reaction to a physical attack might be considerably different from a knee-jerk reaction because you have **learned** to respond in another way.

We also learn to react to stressful situations through years and years of learned behaviors. We go with what works, and what we often think works really well are reactions we learned as a child.

Hint: they don't always work so well when you are an adult.

Parent, Adult, Child

Remember Transactional Analysis? (Eric Berne) Maybe not, but this little gem has been around long enough that it has become one of those accepted ways we look at interactions. It is actually a very good perspective.

In a nutshell, Transactional Analysis suggests that we (all) interact with others in three primary ways:

> As a parent: prejudicial, critical, and nurturing behaviors

> As a child: impulsive, we use "recordings" of early experiences, creatively

> As an adult: organized, adaptable, intelligent*

*(Eric Berne, the founder of Transactional Analysis and author of *Games People Play* – my introduction to Transactional Analysis was from the book, *Born to Win,* by James and Ward; Charles Keating in his book,

37

Dealing with Difficult People, has some excellent sections and discussion on using Transactional Analysis.)

How we fit into Transactional Analysis

We all use each of these **approaches** in our daily lives. While it may seem that ideally we would always want to be in an adult state, the other states do have their uses.

For example:

> It is sometimes great to be like a **child** again, or to enjoy the world from a child-like perspective. It keeps us from being too serious about life and allows us the freedom to explore the world in new ways.
>
> There are also times throughout our day or week, where constructive criticism is warranted and useful (**parent**). And from a parental standpoint, we always want to be as nurturing of others as possible.

How difficult people fit into TA

Using Transactional Analysis to help describe difficult people-ism is a useful tool. Generally, difficult people tend to use the 'parent' approach in a very judgmental way, and also often use a childish (as opposed to child-like) approach in dealing with and reacting to others, i.e. they attempt to solve their problems, needs, and desires with long-outdated childish behaviors.

Where you want to be

In order to maintain our self-control and to respond responsively in difficult situations with difficult people, ideally, we should use an **adult** approach – organized, adaptable, intelligent. However, it is also valuable to use aspects of the **parent** and **child** in our dealings with difficult people. We will talk at some length about 'kindfrontation' (parent) as a choice instead of confrontation and the use of creativity and humor (child) as well as we discuss working through difficult people concerns.

Responding

The word **reacting**, the way we use it here, infers that we lack control over our responses to others. We need to move from **reacting** to **responding** in our interactions with difficult people. This helps give us personal control in the situation and also keeps us from giving over control to another.

Choices

The previous chapters have emphasized the importance of understanding that you have choices in how you react/respond in difficult situations. By working on some of the ideas in those chapters you can develop the self-control and the self-confidence to move from simply **automatically reacting** to difficulties to **choosing your response**.

It is possible!

…but not always easy. As indicated previously, even when we think about our nemesis difficult person, we often have lots of not-so-good feelings arise. Taking the time to pay attention and step back mentally at the beginning of an interaction with a difficult person can make all the difference in whether you are in control enough to **choose** a response.

> **Catch** the thought/emotion/reaction,
>
> **Check it** – think about the choices you have
>
> Then you have the opportunity to **Change it** – to make a different, better choice for you!

Remember

You can only change yourself; you cannot change other people... directly.

> **You can change them by changing your uncontrolled reactions to controlled responses.**
>
> **You can change them by adding positivity to the mix.**
>
> **You can change them by responding in positive ways that they don't expect.**

Practice makes perfect

This is something you can practice in your mind. It is something you can practice every time you interact with difficult people and you can even practice this with everyone. Being in control of who you are and what you bring to any interaction can be learned.

It is particularly useful to practice this (mentally and emotionally) when you encounter strangers. Those difficult 'someones' you have never met before but somehow seem to manage to get in your face or space: like idiots on the road, people who cut in line, etc. This is not easy to do, because we often don't expect any difficulty from someone we don't know; and when it happens, it shocks us. We also want to be 'right' because this person is being unfair and we ARE 'right,' i.e. the other person does not have the right to cut in line. It is very hard to give up the feeling/need to be right, but sometimes it is the wise thing to do. [And it can be the kind thing to do if the person is someone you interact with on a regular basis.]

We often don't know what to do or how to respond in these types of situations. If you can learn to develop the kind of spontaneous **self-control** that allows you to catch yourself before you react, you have developed some very useful and powerful skills.

You can practice this technique and learn to pay attention to your emotions and thoughts; examine what is going on internally; and make a conscious choice not to react as you normally would to these negative intrusions. If the situation is really triggering your hot buttons, you can still make the effort not to react; and just 'be with' your feelings – acknowledging them, feeling them, letting go of them as you realize you still have a choice. As you develop this technique you will recognize that you still can be in control, even though emotionally you want to react outwardly.

You always have a choice

The more you practice making choices, the more you will really buy into this. And to be successful with difficult people, you have to be willing and able to make new choices.

> **Catch it**
>
> **Check it**
>
> **Change it**

Questions/ideas for contemplation

Try stepping back and making a new choice in an interaction with another person today. If you feel the strong urge to react, try to control it, acknowledge your feelings and thoughts, deal with it internally, and choose a more positive response.

Afterward, take note of how you did and how things progressed. Plan to make personal adjustments the next time if you feel they are needed.

Chapter 9

How do you really feel about yourself?

How you treat yourself does have a major impact on your interactions with others. **Treat yourself kindly.**

Knowing Yourself

In essence this whole section of the book has been about knowing yourself. Here we want to take this a step further and talk about how you are treating yourself. If you are not treating yourself well, you have more work to do.

Self-talk

Far too often we tend to be very self-critical. This is manifested in our own self-talk. An excellent exercise, that should become a regular practice in your repertoire of self-improvement work, is **to pay attention to your self-talk**. See if you can focus throughout your day on what kind of feedback, encouragement, criticisms, and judgments you are making toward yourself. [In the process you will also start paying attention to what you are thinking of others – which is also very useful.]

Do this for several days to start, then extend it for several weeks. It takes practice to catch yourself putting yourself down. If you keep it going, it will become a positive habit.

Catch it

We all say negative things to ourselves. When we make a mistake we might say reactively, "You idiot," or "Can't you ever get anything right?" or we might even swear at ourselves.

> Or one of my favorites, since I tend to be 'occasionally' absentminded: "Duh, you forgot the/your _____ (coat, flashlight, drink glass, etc.) you idiot (or something stronger)."

> Which I have learned to temper with the thought, "Well, at least I get more exercise this way," as I climb the many steps in our house for the umpteenth time that day going after something I forgot.

Little lapses are probably excusable. What is not excusable and what can be very detrimental to how we feel and how we come across to everyone we interact with, is when we regularly put ourselves down because we really don't believe in ourselves: our own abilities, our intellect, etc.

For example:

> You may say to yourself on a regular basis something like the following:

> "I never get anything right; what an idiot."

> The truth is, you "almost never get anything wrong." Yes, you do occasionally get things wrong, but by and large you are intelligent, on top of things, and in spite of how some other idiot treats you, you don't have to treat yourself badly.

Start treating yourself kindly and positively. You will find that your attitude will start to shift and you will enjoy life more.

Have courage; be willing to ask

Sometimes it takes another person to be very frank with us to show us how much we deprecate ourselves. It also takes courage to ask another person how we are coming across to others. Both of these are very much tied together.

An interesting truth: I believe that if we tend to be critical of ourselves, that we also have a tendency to be critical of others. Unfortunately, it actually becomes a part of who we are.

A long time ago, I asked a dear friend and colleague how I was coming across to others. She was honest, as I had asked her to be, thankfully in a kind way. I was shocked, to say the least at some of the things she told me. It was a major turning point in my life. It was when I started to turn my 'moodiness' around.

You CAN change

On another occasion, I saw another close friend whom I hadn't seen in years. It was on an occasion when I was giving a speech and he was so astounded at what I was saying, the 'who' I had become since we had last spent time together, that he blurted out right in the middle of the speech (luckily it was a small group of people we all knew), "Boy, Koob, have you changed!" I took that as a compliment (which he later confirmed).

Self-blame

Often, far too often, we accept blame that really isn't ours. This is something that we can 'inherit' from our difficult people. They are good at assigning blame and shame to others and we do tend to take it on if we are not in an assertive, self-confident, positive, self-control mode. Eventually we manifest this in continually blaming ourselves.

Blame leads to guilt and shame

Accepting blame, especially over long periods of time can lead to a great deal of inner feelings of guilt and shame. Yes, we all probably have done things we could feel guilty about until the end of time, but it does not help us or anyone else for us to stuff it and then keep bringing it back up every time someone decides to dish out some more blame, guilt, and shame. Let it go! Permanently!

Back to the Past

Often our feelings of blame, shame, and guilt come from a long history of being told we were worthless, not good enough, idiots, stupid, and the like. If you have had enough of this type of feedback in your life, you begin to believe it and accept it as gospel.

This book is far too short to delve into trying to do something about our negative past. This type of work is best done with professional support. However, being **aware** of our negative self-talk can be the beginning of making huge changes in our lives. I know – been there, done that, still doing that. **Self-work is a continual growth process that can give us more positivity and personal power in our lives.**

Positive self-talk

Recognizing our negative self-talk is the first step toward changing it. You CAN turn it around. It takes sincere dedication and lots of practice.

You need to start talking inwardly to yourself, especially when you catch yourself thinking negative thoughts.

"I AM good enough."

"I AM a worthwhile person."

"I make many intelligent decisions every day."

By observing your negative self-talk, you can get the impetus and ideas for your positive self-talk.

Turn it around!

If you say to yourself, "You idiot," change it to, "I am not an idiot. I am a smart person; I just made a mistake. I will fix it and do better next time." And so on.

If you do this regularly and keep at it, when you look back some time in the future you will find that you have made a difference in your life. You will be adding many more drops of crystal pure water to your beaker and fewer gunky drops. [See Chapter 5]

Worry

Worry is negative self-talk. Worry adds gunky, yucky, sludgy water to your beaker.

Worry does not do ANYONE, leastwise YOU, any good. And it sends a loud and clear message to anyone within range that you are not a happy camper. It does rub off on others, even if you think you are keeping it to yourself.

Sometimes worriers say to me, "But I am trying to plan ahead, to be ready for the worse exigency."

My response is: that it is good to plan ahead, but you don't have to feel bad doing it!

A good exercise

I have found that by far the best exercise for dealing with things we are concerned about, things that we tend to worry about, is to write – Write down all your thoughts about this specific concern and keep writing until you have said everything you can. Then keep writing and see where it leads.

Come back to this later and read it and then write some more.

This process is not only cathartic, it seems that physically putting our concerns into words on paper helps to make them more concrete, easier to understand, and easier to deal with. You are taking something that you are reacting to and becoming active with it. You make a difference. You may even find that as you write, ideas and potential solutions come to mind.

Try this process; it can be very productive and very powerful.

Wow!

You really don't have to feel bad about yourself or the world in general. One of my favorite mantras:

"If you are not having fun, there is something wrong."

(Koob, *A Perfect Day: Guide for a Better Life*)

If you are not having fun...Adjust.

After all, it is your **choice**. Choose wisely; choose for the fun of it!

Questions/ideas for contemplation

If you look deep within yourself, what is the persona you want to bring to world? It would even help to take the time to describe this in writing. The better you envision this, the more likely you will move toward it. Bring your true self to the fore. You will be glad you did and so will others.

[See Appendix I for an excellent exercise that I originally devised for my book, *Guiding Children*. It will help you get at **your truth**.]

Another great exercise:

The penny jar: Put a penny (dime, quarter, dollar) in a jar for every thought you have that is self-deprecatory. This is a good start toward paying attention to yourself!

Donate the money to charity after a month.

You will really start to notice your negative thoughts when you see that stack of dollar bills growing!

Chapter 10

Learning from Difficult People

Difficult People can be our best teachers

Everything you have learned in this book so far is a direct result of your interest in and probably your encounters with difficult people. You can learn a great deal from difficult people.

Much of your valuable education about working and interacting with people has come from the difficult people who have come into your life. The fascinating part is that we all have a great deal more to learn.

Maybe that is why all these difficult people keep showing up in our lives.

Here we go again!

Got a difficult person-type that keeps showing up in your life? Perhaps they are there for a reason. You may or may not feel this way, but it is possible that you have something you need to learn from them. In any case, if this learning opportunity keeps showing up, why not make the most of it and get past this bump in the road?

What not to do

Perhaps the greatest lessons we can learn from difficult people is **how NOT to behave**. Check yourself next time you are in a difficult situation and see if you are behaving like the person you are with; or are you in control and stepping back and behaving the way you want to behave. Are you being the person (persona) you really want to be in this life?

If not, you probably can learn form the situation and the difficult person you are interacting with.

What to do

By imagining and using the inverse of what we are experiencing from a difficult person, we can learn what to do. We can learn how to treat people better, kinder, more gently. We can become a positive force in the universe and not a negative one.

> If someone is being rude and boorish – **learn to be kind**, even when you feel the need to be in control and 'right.'

> If someone uses anger as a tool – **learn to use calmness and peace instead**.

46

If someone uses blame and shame to control others – **learn to support and encourage** as a far better way to deal with people.

If someone uses behind-the-back, surreptitious tactics with others – **learn to bring things out in the open and practice honesty and kindness with everyone**.

Take any negative affect and behavior and you can find the truth and positivity in some other approach that is diametrically the opposite.

The learning just keeps coming

We can learn a tremendous amount about ourselves, about others, and about humanity in dealing with difficult people. It takes our being willing to **open ourselves to the possibilities** and it takes paying attention to ourselves and others – positive attention.

We learn best from experience

As you know difficult people often seem to create numerous experiences for us to learn in. By paying attention, you WILL learn a great deal. Go with the flow.

"Difficult people impel us to rise to the occasion." (Rosen)

Heck, they impel us into motion. The important concept here is to make sure the motion we are starting is in a positive direction – for us and them.

One great perspective

If you take this concept of willingness to be open and to learn from others into your difficult situations with your difficult person, you have automatically changed your whole perspective. You have changed the whole tenor of what will happen. You set a different stage upon which the play will unfold.

Learning is about curiosity, finding out something new, gaining information, and gaining knowledge and wisdom. Using a learning approach to a difficult person helps you see things in a totally new light.

I have done this recently and I find that I now focus on what there is to learn from the experience much more; and focus much less on negativity, bad feelings, negative reactions, and so on. This perspective helps me **maintain control**, which in turn helps me to build **self-confidence** and **self-worth**, which in turn helps me to **respond** in an **assertive** rather than aggressive or passive way.

All that from a little change in perspective.

What comes our way

Is there a reason you have a difficult person in your life?

This is a good question to ask yourself occasionally.

Whatever the case, you do have the opportunity to be educated by everyone you meet. It is a great way to approach difficult people.

Don't be afraid to ask

Ask yourself what you could be learning. Then keep you eyes and ears open.

Questions/ideas for contemplation

What did you learn today from the people in your life? From a difficult person who came your way?

Use these experiences to learn: about yourself, and about others.

Chapter 11

Caring for Yourself

Self-Worth vs Egotism

In my book, *A Perfect Day: Guide for a Better Life*, one very important concept I discuss is "Love yourself and others." Perhaps a better word is "Caring."

Hint:

You can't care for others, unless you feel good about yourself.

Unless you <u>care</u> for yourself.

Egotism is trying to prove you are significant or important.

Self-Worth is Knowing you ARE significant

and being content with that

(Meier and Koob)

When we get past having to prove ourselves to others, having to be right, having to be better than they are, we release a tremendous amount of stuff that can exacerbate difficult situations. As a matter-of-fact, all that stuff can exacerbate life in general.

YOU are significant!

You are here; therefore, you are significant to the universe, at least from my humble perspective.

Accepting our uniqueness, our significance, is no small task because we are too often spending all of our time trying to bolster our constantly flagging egos. Our egos need constant upkeep; and the more we work at it, the more they demand of us. Try letting go of your need for ego and accepting who are.

The true YOU!

If you pause and think deeply about the type of person you truly would like to be, i.e. the qualities you would like to have and the values that are truly important to you, that is the true you. That is the person you need to care about. That is the real you that you need to bring to the fore. Unlike our

49

ego, that person is easy to accept and makes no demands on you, because you are perfect just the way you are. [See Appendix I for a great exercise that helps you discover the values and qualities that speak the most to who you want to be.]

Be kind to yourself

Always be kind to yourself. It helps your own growth and it helps you in your interactions with others. The better you treat yourself; the better you will treat others. Find ways every day to treat yourself well.

Treat yourself

Some advice I have seen in a wide variety of books from the self-help genre to the difficult people genre, point out this simple, but important, idea. **Take time to treat yourself** once in a while. Take time to treat yourself in small ways, every day. It can be something as simple as taking a very brief break from daily stresses, e.g. two minutes to close your eyes, a moment for some positive imagery, or some nice deep, calming breathes.

Try doing something more momentous for yourself occasionally, as well:

> Buy yourself a present, something you have always wanted but never got
>
> Take a half day off and go to the movies or go shopping
>
> Spend time 'you can't afford' with a loved one without any guilt
>
> Buy yourself flowers (or a power tool)
>
> Have an ice cream cone
>
> And so on.

Treat others, too

When you treat others, you treat yourself. **I know of no better feeling than doing something nice for another person.** It comes back many-fold in benefits.

Here is a great example

In a town where I formerly lived, I regularly frequented a local grocery store. One of the checkout ladies was always, and I mean always, cheerful, friendly, and had a nice big smile for me. Just her overall demeanor made me feel good, and made me feel even better when I was having a less than ideal day.

Once, when I had come in the day after having had sinus surgery, she bolstered my spirits by being her usual friendly self. The next time I came in, a few days later, she remembered I had been through surgery and asked how I was doing with the post-op. She showed me kindness, caring, and concern.

A day shortly thereafter, again back at the same store, I spontaneously picked up one of those bouquets of flowers near the checkout. After she had rung up my groceries and the flowers, I handed them back to her and thanked her for being so friendly and kind. She was flabbergasted and a big crocodile tear ran down her cheek. She came around the counter and gave me a big grandmotherly hug.

Was I rewarded? A thousand-fold! I will remember her happy, kind, teary face for the rest of my life.

> "Determine in your heart to sing your own song." (Meier)

> Sing what is in your heart and you will add great joy to others.

Questions/ideas for contemplation

What positivity can you bring to the world this day?

What is your song? Are you singing it? Today?

> "Practice random and anonymous acts of kindness."

I have seen this in numerous locations and in various forms, including bumper stickers. My thanks to whoever originated this great idea.

Part II

Understanding Difficult People

Chapter 12

Difficult People?

Definitions of a difficult person

Difficult people are motivated by fear.

"They are insecure and lack confidence.

They worry about having enough attention, recognition, and control."
(Crowe)

"A truly difficult person – one whose behavior *regularly* interferes with your ability to get along with him or her and/or get your work done effectively or on time." (Weiss)

A difficult person is one whose selfish thoughts or behavior can

ultimately harm someone. Self-centeredness. (Meier)

Any person who causes angst* in the life of another. (Koob)

*distress, anxiety, unease, turmoil, disquiet, tumult, upset, agitation, perturbation [Whew!]

But that means...

I am a difficult person. You are a difficult person. We are all difficult people...at times. You bet.

As much as we would like to be perfect, always in control, always nice people, inadvertently we all cause perturbation in others. And they all cause us to be perturbed too… at times.

Here is another way of looking at it: even Mother Theresa, by all accounts a living Saint in her days on earth, was probably **SEEN** as difficult by other people. **It is all in the eyes of the beholder – it often is!**

Another truth about 'difficultness' is that **if you see someone else as being difficult, it is highly likely they will see you as being difficult**. This is even true of a person who just about everyone sees as difficult. It is probably MOST true about REALLY difficult people.

That also means...

There are, in a sense, degrees of difficulty. As you might imagine they are tough to delineate.

Many authors who have worked in this area have different ways of describing difficult people, or levels of difficult people-ism. I'm going to break this down into three degrees or levels, but please understand from the get-go that these just give us a perspective from which to discuss difficult behaviors in people. In the final analysis, it is simply about how we perceive someone else and how they affect or impact us.

First level difficult people

> You, me, and most of the rest of us

First level difficult people are occasionally difficult. We mean well; we try our best; but somehow, we have our foibles, our differences, our little ways of irritating others. We don't mean to get in another person's way, but it happens sometimes. We make mistakes (ever do something dumb in traffic while driving?); and we certainly do cause angst in others' lives on occasion.

Second level difficult people

This is where you might want to start actually using the phrase 'difficult person.' Second level difficult people are pretty regular in their difficult behavior. They often come across to others in a negative way and they affect more than just a few people adversely on a regular basis. We might even go so far as to use some pretty strong language to describe these difficult people (we won't mention those terms here).

The amazing thing is that second level difficult people often have absolutely no idea they are difficult. I know this is hard to believe, but it is another common characteristic of difficult people. They don't have a clue about how they affect others or how pervasive their negativity is.

I have been in the close vicinity of some VERY difficult second stringers and some of them don't seem to have a clue at how they come across. Even the few who do recognize their tendency to be difficult or seen as difficult by others, really probably didn't mean to be difficult. It is just hard for them to control it and they often feel guilty afterward.

Third level difficult people

First let me qualify this level by saying that I have met only a few truly malicious people in my life, and I am not even sure about that. Third level difficult people **purposely hurt other people**. They roll over others without any consideration of their humanity. They add a tremendous amount of negativity and perturbation to the world, and they don't (at least on a surface level) seem to care about the fact that they are hurting others.

I remember watching an HBO special about someone who struck me as a real possible third level difficult person. His nickname was 'the Iceman' and he was a hitman (killer) for the mob. He had murdered numerous people in horrible ways and in cold blood. He showed no remorse whatsoever. Was he truly evil? Was he a 'classic' malicious difficult person?

Are their truly evil people?

This is a question sometimes asked about difficult people. I personally don't have the answer, but my gut feeling is "No." Or maybe I just want to think the answer to this question is 'No." People typically are the way they are for good reasons (to them). How they were treated in the past and the many stresses they suffered on the road to where they are in life, may have changed them in ways that you and I find it hard to comprehend.

However, as a case in point, while watching this HBO special on the aforementioned 'Iceman,' I was surprised to see that he suddenly became very remorseful and was wiping tears from his eyes when he talked about the angst that he had caused his family. My read on that was, that in spite of all the evidence to the contrary, there was still a part of him that was human. He had just driven the rest of his humanity somewhere into the depths of his being.

The real truth

Most of us can learn to cope, deal, work, win, and be successful with first and second level difficult people. We may even be successful with a truly malicious person; however, if you encounter or deal with such a person, my advice would be to be positive, kind, compassionate, and honest, and then remove yourself from the situation as quickly as possible. Discretion sometimes is the better part of valor.

From my standpoint as a coach, counselor, educator, manager, father, and general all-around human being, my best guess is that most of us fit into first level difficult people-ism. A small minority of folks, are second level difficult people, and a very, very small minority, thankfully, are third level difficult people.

Hopefully you will never encounter a third level difficult people that you have to live or work with.

THE most important point

We will focus in this book on **difficult behaviors**, not difficult people. Difficult people exhibit or use, difficult behaviors (unconsciously or consciously) because it is how they fill their needs, wants, and desires. Calling someone a difficult person labels them and takes away from their wholeness as a person.

NEVER call someone a difficult person. Sometimes we do, however, have to call their attention to their difficult behavior.

The rest of the story

(And a Hat tip to Paul Harvey)

We are going to spend a fair amount of time discussing general characteristics of difficult people behavior. In the third Section of this book, we will discuss more specific difficult behaviors and how you can be successful when interacting with people who exhibit these behaviors.

Caution

This book does not address difficulties with people who have serious personal problems: alcoholics, drug addicts, seriously mentally disturbed people, fanatics, and abusers. First, I would not even begin to try to categorize them as to their level of difficult people-ism. While some of the techniques herein may work with them, if and when you may have to deal with these types of people concerns, there is something beyond anyone's control that is affecting their interactions with you and others. They need to get help.

Important: It is a tough personal decision as to whether or not you should help them find the help they need.

Very important: Please, unless you are a qualified professional with appropriate training, do NOT try to self-diagnose someone else. Leave this to qualified professionals.

Most important: Take care of yourself and others. When in doubt in any difficult situation, get help or get out if there is ever any threat of serious escalation or violence.

Questions/ideas for contemplation

Spend a few moments thinking about the difficult people in your life and try to separate the **behavior** from the person. When you can do this, you can look at the person's humanity first and deal with what you feel is an inappropriate behavior as a separate issue.

Can you think of some ways that perhaps you cause angst in another's life?

This is a good learning exercise. You could start with:

"People get upset when I…."

Or,

"I upset (frustrate, anger) people when I…"

This can be an eye-opening process and will help you further along on your path of self-discovery.

Note: my book, *Me, a Difficult Person*, focuses on learning more about how we come across to others, and skills and techniques we can use to become a kinder, gentler, more compassionate human being. It also gives further insight into difficult people and difficult behaviors in general.

Chapter 13

The Seven Keys to Being Successful with Difficult People

These seven key ideas are the backbone of the materials presented throughout this site. I developed these after extensive research, study and experience relevant to difficult people and difficult situations. As you begin to understand more about dealing successfully with difficult people come back to these Key Ideas. You will find they offer a tremendous amount of insight.

As you work on your understanding and strengths in these important areas you will notice a marked difference and improvement in how you perceive 'difficult' people, how you interact with them, and how you handle their 'difficult' interpersonal behaviors.

These *Seven Keys* are centered in your **attitude about yourself and others.**

Working successfully with other people centers around how we feel about ourselves. Their 'stuff' has a direct effect on how they interact with us, but does not have to affect how we feel or go about our own work. When we can step beyond their problems and live our life to the fullest, making the most of our work on OUR terms; we have learned to truly be in control.

The Seven Keys to Being Successful with Difficult People

Self-awareness

Self-worth

Self-confidence

Self-control

Honesty

Kindness

Positivity

Self-awareness

Self-awareness tops this list because it is fundamental to all the other ideas. **When we begin to understand ourselves better, we can make better choices, and we strengthen our self-worth, self-confidence, and self-control.** There is no better tool available for you to help build your foundation for dealing effectively and positively with others.

57

Working on your self-awareness pays big dividends. It is helpful to start this process by reading more extensive materials on how to develop these skills. [See *Me! A Difficult Person?*, and *A Perfect Day: Guide for a Better Life*, (Koob)]

Self-worth

Self-worth is how we value ourselves. It has nothing to do with ego – which is placing ourselves above others. It has to do with who we truly believe ourselves to be and how we bring that to the world. It has to do with understanding **our most fundamental values**; the person we would most like to be to and with others.

Self-confidence

As we develop our self-worth, our self-confidence improves. Many of the difficulties we have with other people are affected a great deal by our inability to **maintain a confident and positive demeanor** when we are with them. You can be assured that if you are getting upset, defensive, depressed, etc. that your confidence is taking a hit.

Assertiveness is being able to accept yourself in an interaction with another person regardless of their behavior. It does take practice and self-awareness.

Self-control

Control of other people is an illusion. It is an illusion that drives difficult people to their difficult behaviors. To be successful with difficult people our only recourse is **self-control**. We are not out to control them, only our own feelings, thoughts, and responses to their difficult behaviors. **When we are in-control, they almost always don't have any choice but to change their negative behavior when interacting with us.**

No one can control our lives without our permission! We always have positive choices we can make. Sometimes they are difficult to understand or to see. Practice in self-awareness, awareness and understanding of others, and in developing our self-worth and self-confidence can make all the difference.

Honesty

Honesty means being honest with ourselves (more self-awareness!) and being **kindly honest** with others.

You always have a right to be honest with others and there are ALWAYS positive ways to do that.

Kindness

Every interaction we have with other people has the opportunity for us to be kind, or to be something else. Practicing kindness, especially in the face of difficult behavior, pays huge dividends. Try it! You will be pleasantly surprised.

It can be really tough to be kind and compassionate in the face of a very disagreeable, inflexible person. Try to keep in mind that this difficult person is a child of the universe no less than you. Whatever 'stuff,' past and current, has them where they currently are, is perhaps quite unfortunate, for you, and especially for them. You may be able to make a positive difference to their existence, even if it is only for a short time. And **you may very well be the catalyst that helps them start to turn their life around.**

Positivity

This can be summed up in one of Dr. Koob's favorite sayings:

Negativity breeds Negativity

Positivity Breeds Positivity

Choose Wisely

Another way to say this is:

Negativity NEVER helps!

And that pretty much says it all. We always can choose to be positive, even in the face of negativity. When we do make the right choice, we have the opportunity to help change someone else's day, week, maybe even their life, around. Wow!

Questions and Ideas for Contemplation

Keep *The Seven Keys* handy: print them out, laminate them, keep a small version in your wallet, pocketbook. Reminding yourself of these is very important in your self-help work through difficult situations.

Even more important: practice working with these, especially **Self-awareness**, which is the foundation for the others. Becoming more self-aware is a life's work. It is well worth the effort!

Chapter 14

Differences

**Differences between people can be the catalyst
for difficult situations**

We are ALL different!

Often difficult situations arise because of how we (me, you, and our difficult people) look at the world. In the next few chapters, we are going to look at people in general, as well as the differences that can cause difficulties to arise between them.

A key to working with other people throughout your life is being **willing to make an attempt to look at the world from their standpoint.** It helps you **understand what is perhaps motivating their behavior**. The better you understand their world, the better you can learn to work with them and be successful with them.

It is helpful to keep in mind that they may not always be willing to understand your slant on things. However, your openness can still make a difference. **When you open up communications with a person and show a willingness to understand who they are and where they are coming from, you change the dynamics of your relationship with them in a positive direction.** You may not become best buddies, but you may reach a point where the tolerance of differences is accepted on both sides of the aisle.

Perspectives

We have already talked at some length about what you are bringing to the party. The other person is also bringing a tremendous amount of 'stuff' along with them. Their stuff is likely very different from your stuff. What works for you, probably does not work for them. Your task, and it is not always an easy one, is to try to understand what is motivating the way they are acting and reacting.

How?

We do this through careful observation, i.e., paying attention to them, listening carefully, and through skillful communication. These areas will be discussed at some length as they are critical to your success with difficult people.

First, we are going to explore some general ways of looking at difficult behaviors and the differences in people that are often at the root of those behaviors.

Labeling

We all label other people. It may be something as simple as, "She's a blond," with the subconscious caveat, 'I really like blonds.' Or, "He has a beard," with, 'I hate to kiss men with beards' attached. These probably seem silly, but we make these kinds of judgments/labels all the time. When they get in our way in our interactions with others, from either side of the fence, problems can arise and they can quickly become a thorn in the side that dooms the relationship.

What often happens with people with whom we are having difficulties is that a single bad habit, foible, lapse in judgment on their part (or even our part) can set up a perspective that stays with us or them forever. We label the other person based on whatever we associate with them. If this irritating behavior is repeated, or regular, it becomes a permanent fixture in our perception of them.

We lose the whole person because we focus on things that might not be that important.

Labeling is a form of highlighting differences between people.

Know thyself

We have discussed knowing yourself, but do you know what it is about YOU that is causing the other person angst? Remember, an important concept that we noted earlier is that **if we see a person as difficult it is very likely they see US as being difficult**, too. So looking at the world through their glasses can tell you a whole bunch about why you are both having difficulties with each other.

It does not hurt to ask

Here is an early technique:

> Because you have learned to come to a conversation with self-confidence, self- control, and the ability to listen to criticism (even if it is not justified) without reacting negatively, it can be helpful to ask a difficult person in your life why your relationship with them is so rocky.

> This approach gives them the lead and a sense of control (which is probably part of what they want or need), but **it is okay to do this because you are in control of you**. It is VERY important to listen carefully and not get defensive – remember that the idea is for you

to learn something about yourself, and more importantly, to learn how they perceive you.

Don't respond until they have finished. You can encourage them to continue, but let them have their say, even if you feel they have a completely unfair perspective of who you are.

You might be surprised at the doors this simple technique will open and this might be the start toward getting past the difficulties that were blocking your relationship in the past.

Know others

The technique above will tell you as much about them as it does you. You don't have to agree with anything they say and you may find that they will be unwilling to tell you anything, but it could be worth a try. Just your effort says to them. "I want to change this relationship for the better." It may be the start of moving this relationship in the right direction; and you have accomplished that without blame by giving them something they want anyway – positive attention, plus a sense of control.

Some things you might find out:

> Their perception of you is diametrically opposite, or vastly different from how you see yourself

> They are biased about something about you – physically, socially, how you act, etc

> There has been some misunderstanding between you both

> You really do see things (perhaps many things) differently, but you have at least opened the door for understanding these differences

> You come across to them (and perhaps to others) far differently than you thought – this can open your eyes, too, so that if you want to make personal adjustments, you can

> Many other things – you are trying to open the door to communicating with them on a different level; listen and learn if they are willing to share with you.

At all costs avoid reacting negatively, blaming, judging them, pointing your finger back at them, etc. Be open to what they say, and respond encouragingly and politely.

> "John, I appreciate everything you are telling me. I didn't understand how you felt and it makes a difference to me to understand your perspective. Thank you."

Always **thank them** for their willingness to be open and honest with you. You may not like what they say, and you may disagree with their perceptions, but if you are on top of your game, you can use this to understand yourself and them even better.

> "Wow, thanks for sharing that, John. I really don't see myself that way, but it is important for me to understand how you feel. Could you tell me a bit more about why you feel I am _______?

We are going to spend a good bit of time on communications, but the better you know your 'opponent' the easier all this becomes. Everything you read in the next few chapters is focused on **a better understanding of difficult people: how they think, work, react; what is important to them; and what their intent is**. Always keep in mind the following key points when communicating:

> **Keep it positive** in spite of how they are acting
>
> **Never blame**, even if they are blaming you
>
> **Listen** – it shows respect and helps the other person feel in-control
>
> **Be calm, open, in-control, and self-confident**
>
> **Thank them** for their willingness to be open, regardless of their demeanor

Beyond labeling: biases

We all have biases. Difficult people may have more biases than 'normal.' They may be really set in their ways, and unwilling to change their perspective of the world and others. Still, understanding can help you make better choices; and it will give you a foundation for knowing how to deal with this person more successfully.

Biases are a more intense form of labeling. You have probably heard the expression, "He is set in his ways." A person can be biased toward you because you smoke, have red hair, are overweight or too thin, are an authority figure, and so on. Jealousy may be a part of intense biases by another person.

Biases are hard to change, but if you know the other person has them and what they are, it helps you to understand why they are behaving in a difficult manner towards you or others. Knowledge is always a powerful tool.

Beyond biases: prejudices

We all know what prejudices are. We have all seen or encountered prejudiced people. Like everything else about people, you cannot change a person who is prejudiced. Sometimes you just have to work around their unfortunate perspective of the world, other people, you. However, you do have the right to **stand up for yourself**. Hopefully you can do that **self-confidently and in a non-defensive, kind-frontational way**. We will discuss some techniques for dealing with biases and prejudices later in the book. Keep in mind, however, that there are always positive ways we can be assertive about who we are and how we are treated.

Sexual Harassment and other legal issues

Sexual harassment is a legal issue. There are also other relational situations where a legal course of action may be the only recourse you have, e.g. abuse of all forms. If things have gone this far, get help. Please! You are a child of this universe, you deserve to live and work in peace.

[See Dr Koob's work Trilogy: *Succeeding at Work*, which includes, *Succeeding with Difficult Coworkers*; *Succeeding with Difficult Bosses*; and *Managing Difficult Employees* for discussions on dealing with Harassment issues. These are all available at Amazon.com for Kindle and in Paperback.]

Acknowledge differences...

and accept them. They add a richness to life. When you are able to acknowledge, accept, and even appreciate the differences in others, you are raising your own humanity. People will appreciate your understanding and acceptance.

Sometimes that is all they were after in the first place.

Questions/ideas for contemplation

Try making a list of differences between you and a difficult person in your life. You might be surprised at how this effort brings you a better understanding of each of you and of them. It can also give you a quiet confidence the next time you interact with this person.

What are some of the labels you find yourself placing on other people? Try writing these out and then spend some time considering how these perspectives might influence your communications with them. This is a really good way to know yourself better.

Chapter 15

Personality Types

"How does your difficult person perceive life?" (Crowe)

This is an excellent question to ask yourself when you are dealing with someone on a regular basis who tends to get on your nerves.

Talk about labeling! Psychiatrists and psychologists and related professionals (I was going to say 'related ilk' but some of them might have thought I was being difficult!) have been trying to place us into neat little personality categories ever since Freud and Jung (and before!).

These psychological personality categorizations do have validity and some of them are quite interesting and worthwhile. You could take one or two of these types of scales/tests and see where you seem to fit into the scheme of things. You will probably learn a good bit about yourself in the process. You might, however, have trouble convincing a difficult person to take it just for your own edification and understanding.

So if you really want to delve into the world of personality-typing you have lots of choices. Here are a few to start with. [Note: Today many personality inventories can be taken on line.]

Minnesota Multiphasic Personality Inventory

Whew! I would be breathing hard if I had to say that. It is better known as the MMPI and is one of the best-known inventories.

Myers-Briggs Type Indicator

This one is also quite well known. You might be familiar with the categories that people are assessed in:

> extroversion/introversion
>
> sensate/intuitive
>
> thinking/feeling
>
> judging/perceiving

Both of these tests/scales are scientifically tested and considered to be valid and reliable instruments.

Bell/Smith Personality Assessment

This is a personality assessment instrument found in *Winning with Difficult People*, by Arthur Bell and Dayle Smith. I include it here because it is the only one, I have discovered so far that is specifically designed for/with difficult people in mind. Their 'Types' include: The Member, The Self, The Juggler, The Planner, The Thinker, The Empathizer, The Closer, and The Researcher. They use a multiple-choice questionnaire.

Me! A Difficult Person?

The second signature work I wrote for www.difficultpeople.org was a book titled, *Me! A Difficult Person?* I devised a fifty-question scale/test that focuses on behaviors that we and others exhibit that someone might see as difficult. It is not really a personality inventory; more of an attempt to show how a wide variety of behaviors we use can be interpreted differently by different perspectives toward life. [Please note that this test is not a Normed scale. It has not been scientifically validated and its purpose is simply as a personal learning tool.]

Know thyself

I know, I have emphasized this point quite a bit in this book, but the major focal point is that if we learn more about our own personality; and also how we can perceive other people's personalities, perspectives, approaches to life, we have another base of knowledge for being successful in difficult situations.

A word of caution: these tests do produce labels. Use labels wisely. They are 'an indication of,' not necessarily the truth. Given a different day, a different mood, results might be different. I have taken both the MMPI and the Myers-Briggs at least twice each, as well as several other personality inventories. They are very interesting and have given me a perspective of myself I didn't have before.

My approach

How people interact with each other and the world is a fascinating study. I have been contemplating this for many years and, yes, I have my own system. I only have two divisions: "Romantic" and "Classic." These dichotomous (opposite) terms are useful in laying out a **continuum** upon which we can make some general assessments of personality.

Romantic--Classic

I am not sure exactly what got me to thinking along these lines, but here are two distinct possibilities:

> Two excellent books that I read whose central focus is around
> these two perspectives are – *Zen and the Art of Motorcycle
> Maintenance,* by Robert Pirsig and *Narcissus and Goldmund,* by

66

Herman Hesse. I highly recommend these as fascinating reading. They are both an in-depth dissertation, in story form, of this Classic and Romantic dichotomy.

The other possibility is from my teaching, for many years, Romantic Period and Classical Period music history courses. This concept also found its way into my lectures in my Music Appreciation courses. I would have the students supply synonyms for each of these terms as a means of exploring a further understanding of them in relationship to Classical music.

Results of a typical brainstorming session with students would yield the following:

Classic/Classical

Traditional	Structured
Organized	Intellectual
Conservative	Rigid
Classic paintings/art	Neat
and so on.	

Romantic

Free	Freedom
Emotions/emotional	Passion
Liberal	Roses
Sexy	Love
Unstructured	Creative
Intuitive	Messy

and so on. **The continuum**

If you consider this a continuum with the most Classically oriented people on the far right and the most Romantically oriented people on the far left, where would you fit in?

It is a very interesting perspective, because we do often tend to attract opposites into our lives. AND we don't always see ourselves as others see us.

In my classes we used to 'rate' each other and ourselves along a continuum from three C's to two C's over to 3 R's. The results were fascinating for all of us. (I usually fell between one and two R's.)

Interestingly, there were always wide variations in how people saw themselves compared to how others saw them.

Romantic/Classic Continuum

RRR---------RR----------R----------M----------C----------CC---------CCC

M is a theoretical midpoint.

Differences

This 'scale,' and others, are actually about differences between people. For instance: if you are relatively disorganized and unstructured, then a more organized person will look at you askance and be frustrated with you because you don't fit their idea and ideal of the world. Just as, less organized, unstructured-types don't understand why there is so much fuss about keeping things neat. Or if you are a free-thinker, a liberal, you probably don't see eye-to-eye with a real conservative type.

Personality Typing

From whatever perspective you look at it from, personality-typing shows us more about why differences between people make a difference – sometimes BIG differences.

Think about this

It is fairly common for people of opposite personalities to be attracted to each other. Perhaps it is because we want or need someone to complement our own personality. Or maybe the fact that they see the world differently from the way we do has some sort of fascination for us. Or perhaps we see something exotic or exciting in their viewpoint because we don't really understand it.

This is great up to a point, but differences do tend to cause concerns; and when little irritations grow and the honeymoon is over, they can become more serious confrontations. It is not unusual for both people to start seeing each other as difficult.

Ask any couple where one person likes things neat and tidy and their significant other can never seem to put anything away!

Neat versus Messy – a very common cause of angst between two people

Differences in who we are when compared to others is, in my opinion, **the single most important reason we have difficult people problems.**

How they look at you

It is equally as important to understand, if at all possible, **how your difficult person looks at you.** All of this personality stuff goes both ways. You learn more about other people and how they perceive you by keen observation and good communication skills.

Who is going to adjust?

With this basic knowledge you have the opportunity to be understanding, compassionate, and kind in your dealings with the difficult person in your life. **It is not likely that they are going to adjust unless you do.** Whatever techniques you have used in the past probably haven't worked very well. Change yourself, your approach; then there is a good possibility they will change, too.

You now have some very powerful ammo. Use it wisely and compassionately.

Questions/ideas for contemplation

Where do you fit into the personality scheme of things?

Checking this out is a very interesting pursuit. Thinking about it helps you to be more understanding and tolerant of others. It is about our humanity.

Chapter 16

Why are they being difficult?

A Starting Point

"Why are they being difficult?" is a BIG question. We have already looked at a key area: how people are different. We also need to look at what is motivating them.

What can really be a great help in being successful with difficult people is to consider:

>What they **need**
>
>What they **want**
>
>What they **care about**
>
>Their **intent**

We will discuss the first three of these in this chapter and then focus solely on understanding their intent in the next.

Important: When you make a concerted effort to understand what someone needs, wants, and cares about, they will very likely appreciate your efforts, the attention you are paying them, and the respect they feel from you for making this effort.

What do they need?

We are not going to delve very deeply into the psychological make-up of difficult people in this book as it is beyond the scope of what we are trying to accomplish and because "there are as many types of difficult people as there are difficult people." We are all different!

However, there are some general characteristics that can be applied to most difficult people that tend to be fairly universal and go very much to the point of what they need. When you can help fulfill their needs in positive ways, you will have made a major difference in your relationship with them.

Acknowledgment/Acceptance

Often difficult people have a very low self-image or to use an old phraseology, an 'inferiority complex.'* It is fairly common for them not to recognize this in themselves because they will hide it by being dominating, blustery, over-powering or even by being just the opposite, very passive, non-committal, and by avoiding conflict. Their cry for help, **their need, is**

to be accepted, to be acknowledged for who they are. They also could use some basic caring and concern. Unfortunately, their outward behavior creates just the opposite in their lives – it tends to turn people off.

*Inferiority complex is actually a useful and fairly accurate way to look at how the ego tries to build itself by putting others down, trying to maintain control in any and every situation, and by being 'better than.' It goes right to the heart of the conception of how a low self-image affects someone.

If you understand this very powerful need in people, you can help give them what they need and it may be a very effective means of helping them move away from the difficult behaviors they have used in the past.

This seems like an easy solution, and in a sense, it is, BUT it is something you need to do often, and regularly, because the need is great. The payoff for you is that you can quite frequently nip difficult behavior in the bud by getting at the root of one of the reasons they use it – to gain attention. It would not be unusual for a person's difficult behavior to go away completely over time. You are fulfilling one of their most important needs.

Acceptance and **appreciation** often come from **simply paying positive attention to another person**. By listening carefully, asking questions, and making an effort to understand, you can help fill this need. Add occasional compliments, kind words, kudos, and words of appreciation and you may make a tremendous difference in their life and yours.. **It has to start somewhere, and it is not likely to start with them**. Step up to the plate and be the kind, caring catalyst to make this happen – after all it is your relationship, too.

When we can give up our ego and be nice and be kind in spite of what they have said and done, and what they may say and do, we take a step higher on the ladder of humanity. It is worth thinking about!

Being kind and compassionate is always worth the effort. However, there are some REALLY difficult people out there who may not respond as well as you would like to your efforts. It is always your choice to try. Maybe, just maybe, somewhere deep inside they will be affected (infected?) by your positivity.

Need to be right

Find ways to help them be right. Find ways to help them to be successful. You will be way ahead of their game. Remember, "You have a choice between being right and being kind." (Wayne Dyer)

Can you give up your need to be right all the time?

It can be hard to do, but it does work.

Important: most of the time we don't NEED to be right.

71

Keep in mind that many times when we feel the need to be right, our **ego** is kicking in, so that we can feel better than, in-control, more powerful – in other words, we may be being difficult, too.

An example

You and about eight other people are standing in line to check in to a hotel. There are two desk clerks, but only one line, and as one clerk becomes free, the person at the front of the line takes the open position. You have been waiting for about twenty minutes and are now, finally, next to go up. Without a word to anyone and for no apparent reason that you can discern, a man comes in from the side and moves up in front of one of the clerks and waits, completely ignoring the rest of the line. He is dressed in coat and tie and an overcoat that screams 'business establishment.' He seems quite full of himself by the way he moves and the way he acts as if no one else exists.

The person immediately behind you coughs loudly to try to draw his attention, but he does not even glance back. You tap him on the shoulder gently and when he turns and glares at you, rather arrogantly you feel, you say, "Excuse me, sir, but there is only one line and we have all be waiting for a while."

He responds angrily with, "No, there are two lines and I'm next. Now don't bother me again." Then he jerks back to the front placing his back to you and everyone else in the line and mumbles something else that you don't quite catch, but it seems to end with the word, "______ idiots."

If you are like most of us, you will probably start to simmer inside at this jerk's inconsideration and arrogance. You may have even passed the simmer point and are starting to boil.

This is a classic example of where you and the other seven people in line are RIGHT and this guy is wrong. You have every right to stand up for yourself and insist that this guy move to the back of the line.

Consider this: The guy is probably (obviously, perhaps, by his arrogance and attitude) a bully and used to stepping all over other people. You, and anyone else in line with the guts to do it, have every right to make a fuss, to engage the guy in a verbal debate (argument, battle?) over who is right and who is wrong. If your initial impression of him is any indication, he is more than willing to fight to maintain his 'rightness.' (See Chapter 21 for a discussion on being successful with bullies.)

You can choose to be right and engage him, but what will you WIN if you do? Will the three to four minutes you gain by being 'next' be worth the hassle and all the negative feelings that an escalating encounter will bring?

You could also admit to yourself that you are right, make a choice to let go of your need to be right by acknowledging that he has lots of negative 'stuff' going on in his life that you don't need to buy into, and give up all those negative feelings you are having about rightness and fairness and arrogant idiots.

If you choose the latter, you can release the tension and ill will and move on with your life. This guy isn't worth all the fuss and effort. He just isn't.

If you are still having difficulty releasing the need to be right in this type of situation, ask yourself,

> "Are hours, even days of angst worth four minutes of my time?"

> "Is this BULLY worth my aggravation and effort?

This is one of those situations where being right is mostly about ego, and not about the actual need to be right. You won't be giving up anything, really, if you let this rest.

You will not be 'less than' – you will actually be '**more than**' because you have taken the high road to this guy's low road. You are exercising kindness even where it isn't warranted and you ARE taking a step higher on the ladder of what humanity is all about.

> You are not 'giving in' or 'giving up' anything important.

> You are not making him right and you wrong, by being magnanimous – you are just **giving up your ego's need to feel right**.

> You are not 'losing face' or losing your 'honor' – you are being far more honorable than he is. Think about this: what is 'losing face' or 'losing our honor'? What are we losing? Is there some reputation thing at work here?

> Is he really winning anything? Are you really losing anything? Anything important?

Yes, it is very tough to not engage in these types of circumstances. **It takes a good bit of will-power to release this negative energy and to release the need we feel to be right.**

Try stepping back in your mind when you are in a difficult encounter like this and see whether you and/or they have a need to be right. Sometimes this can be a very powerful force and it is extremely difficult to give up this NEED. If you observe this in yourself, you will understand how difficult it is for someone else to let go of the need to be right, too. The guy mentioned above is probably not going to give up his need to be right without a major battle.

Can you examine your motivation to be right and be honest about how important something really is?

Is the world going to change if you are not right?

Is your life going to change dramatically if you give up the need to be right on this issue?

Can you be generous and give up your need to be right, while still maintaining your self-worth and self-respect?

Remember: **the only true form of control is self-control**. Letting someone else be right is not about giving them control; it IS often about being kind. And on the rare occasions when it really does make a difference to be right, can you find ways to be right and kind at the same time? It is possible!

Need to get your attention

Sometimes difficult people are merely trying to get your attention, your undivided attention. Practice your communication skills with difficult people. Learn to listen, really listen and pay attention to what is important to them. All they may really want is to be heard. You don't have to agree with them, just lend them your ear and let them know you are trying to understand their side of things. (See Chapter *18 Communicating with Difficult People*)

Need for attention

This is such a simple solution to some concerns that it is hard to imagine why we don't make more of an effort on a day-to-day basis to pay them some extra attention. However, it is far too often a mistake made by many managers in the busy, helter-skelter world of business today. **Some difficult people simply need attention. Give it to them and your problems with them may be solved.**

> Hint to managers: take a 'walk-about' every day or at least once a week and try to make contact with everyone under you. It will pay huge dividends. Also, keep in mind that some people are needier than others; they may need a little extra attention. People like to be recognized just for being.

Here is an excellent thought:

> "The more critical a person is,

the more desperate is his craving for attention." (Littauer)

Sometimes all we need to do is pay someone some positive attention:

> Send them a quick e-mail at the start of the day

Stop by for a quick hello

Give them a quick call

Let them know that you know they exist; better yet, let them know you appreciate their being there

Pay them a compliment when you see them

There are many ways to show **positive regard** to someone, and it takes very little effort and time. The results to your relationship with them may change dramatically over a period of time if you stick with this type of positive program.

Need for recognition

Again, fairly simple, but far too often we forget to do anything on a regular basis because we are too busy. There are many ways to recognize people. Don't wait until some formal process to do it. Saying 'thank you,' works wonders. You can recognize needy people daily with a kind word and an 'atta-boy'or 'atta-girl.' E-mails can help, but personal contact works wonders. Make it a habit.

Need to be understood

This is a BIG one! It is all about your communication skills – particularly listening carefully, reframing, mirroring, and giving feedback. **Find ways to let them know that they are not only heard, but understood.**

Need to get along

It sure does not seem like they need to get along, does it? Not the way they are acting. Not when they are in your face screaming, or when they seem to completely avoid contact with everyone. However, it is not uncommon for difficult people to feel 'out of it' or 'not a part of.'

Help them to belong.

Help them to understand, by your example – an example that says that there are better ways to get along with others.

Kind words and personal contact can make a major difference to how they see you and how they act within your purview.

Wants

'Wants' are very close to needs, however, there is one important key difference. What they think they want and what they really need, may be entirely different. The best skill you can bring to address this in a difficult situation is **to listen carefully** and to **be willing to ask** them what they want. If you can get them talking about themselves and telling you what all the fuss is about, you will find out what they want. Maybe you can provide it. Even if you can't provide it, you may still find out that just your openness to their sharing what is important to them will solve a great many problems.

Asking is one of the great communication skills you can develop in working with others. When you ask what is important to them, what they want, what they need, etc., **you are showing them respect, attention, and a willingness to understand**. All of these are keys to being successful with difficult people.

They <u>want</u> to not to be afraid

While most difficult people would not be willing to acknowledge it, they are often motivated by fear. Take another look at the needs above and reverse them – those are fears:

> Fear that no one cares
>
> Fear that no one knows who they are or cares about what is important to them
>
> Fear that no one likes them
>
> Fear that no one understands who they are or what they need
>
> Fear that they are not good enough
>
> And so on.

Remember the discussion earlier about fear being the root of all negative emotions?

It is difficult to work with a person's fears directly; and unless you are a certified professional counselor, I wouldn't recommend trying it. But by paying attention to a person's needs, you help reduce their fear. **By understanding that difficult behavior is precipitated by and powered by fear, you have a powerful tool to help other people.**

They <u>want</u> to stop hurting

People who are difficult are hurting inside. Their behavior is motivated by their pain and fear. Through understanding, compassion, support, and your humanity, you can do a great deal to help with this. Through understanding, you can also NOT be party to making their fear and pain worse. You have this power, right now, to make a positive difference – WOW!

What do they care about?

Finding out what people care about helps you to understand them and gives you another tool for being successful with them. Acknowledge what is important to them, respect what is important to them, and support them as you can.

The bonus is that all of this feels good when we make this effort. While you may have to swallow a bit of pride to take that first step, isn't it worth the effort to have a positive, productive relationship with someone rather than a problem relationship?

Positivity breeds Positivity

Choose Wisely

AND,

If you are not having fun – adjust.

Questions/ideas for contemplation

Look at all of these concepts from your own standpoint:

> What needs and wants do you have?

> What do you care about?

> How do these play a role in difficult situations you encounter?

Important: the hardest part of making a commitment to pay more positive attention to someone is getting out of the gate. If your relationship with them has been strained for some time, you understand this as soon as you think about making this effort. Try to keep in mind that even though it will feel awkward at first, and that there may be a great deal of suspicion from them to start with, that if you do make the effort and stick with it, things will most likely change for the better. Isn't this amount of effort worth having a more harmonious relationship?

Chapter 17

Intent

We can go beyond needs, wants, and what difficult people care about by looking at their intent in a difficult situation. An excellent habit to get into when you find yourself in a difficult situation with someone is to ask yourself,

> "What is their intent?"

Or in other words,

> "What do they want here?"

> "What is their purpose" "

> "What are they after?"

Other authors of difficult people books discuss intent, but Dr. Brinkman and Dr. Kirshner have an excellent section in their book, *Dealing with People You Can't Stand.* Below you will find the four 'intents' they delineate in their text. I will discuss these, as they give another perspective toward understanding difficult people. I will also add one of my own.

Perhaps the key point here is that difficult people don't do things in a vacuum. They have a purpose. There is method behind their madness (a nod to Shakespeare). **They are receiving a reward for their behavior.** (Crowe)

Intent

The first four 'intents' below are slightly paraphrased from *Dealing with People You Can't Stand*, Brinkman and Kirshner.

Behavior becomes more...

> **Controlling** when the intent is to **get it done**

> **Perfectionistic** when the intent is to **get it right**

> **Approval-seeking** when the intent is to **get along**

> **Attention-getting** when the intent is to **get appreciated**

> **Difficult** when people **don't care**; when the intent is **to be cared for** (Koob)

Get it done

Some people are driven about getting things done. It is their all-consuming motivation at work and sometimes even at play. They may give up some quality control because their aim is 'get it in, get it out, get it done quickly.' This type of orientation can really frustrate the "get it right" person.

Get it done people often feel that the amount of work they do, the amount they accomplish is what matters most. They could probably use training in revising, editing, and quality control.

Get it right

At all costs! Perfectionists aim at getting things right. They can be so motivated to 'get it right' that they never get anything done, or at the very least it takes them a long time to get something off their desk.

Know any picky people? They probably come from the get it right school.

Get it right people can have a phobia about turning in anything that is less than perfect. They could use help in decision making and moving things along in the pipeline. Let them know that it is safe to get things done (on time).

Get along

We talked about the need to get along in the previous chapter. This is an important consideration when looking at intent, as well. From personal experience and a long study of this topic, I don't think many people want to be known as difficult. Most of us really do want to get along with others and to be seen in a favorable light by everyone else.

One reason it is better to focus on difficult behaviors to understand what is motivating someone's behavior is because very few people are incorrigibly difficult or want to be.

Even though their behavior often says, 'get out of my way,' 'leave me alone,' 'let me do this my way,' or takes other negative forms, many (most?) difficult people really want to get along.

Acknowledgment and acceptance really can help here.

Some 'get along' people put your needs, wants, and cares before their own because they want to be accepted and acknowledged. They try to please everyone. (Brinkman and Kirshcner)

Get appreciated

Everyone wants to be appreciated. With a difficult person, it can be a very demanding need. The more we show our appreciation to/with most difficult people who have this fundamental need, the less difficult behavior they will likely manifest.

Don't stop at acknowledgment and acceptance, appreciate them. Try to appreciate the positive attributes of this type of difficult person often, every day. By focusing on the positive, we begin to see them in a different light. Basic psychology tells us that **what we pay attention to will be reinforced and repeated**.

If our focus is always on the negative,

that is what will continue to happen.

It is worth thinking about this whenever we are dealing with someone who is being difficult. When we can find their positive side and focus on that, we change the dynamics of our relationship with them.

Focus on the positive instead; reinforce that!

To be cared for

I have added this to Brinkman's and Kirschner's list because I feel this is a fundamental intent of almost everyone. It is a fundamental NEED that often is not being met, so we seek it everywhere we can. Caring is, in some ways, synonymous with love.

We all want and need love.

"All we need is love" (Beatles et al)

The word 'love,' unfortunately, tends to have a romantic connotation that seems a bit awkward when talking about any but our closest friends and relatives. **Caring** works better.

If you show concern, genuine caring to another, the odds are they will know that they are receiving a precious gift from you. If you can do this in spite of their being difficult, you are <u>giving yourself</u> a precious gift. Think about it.

Knowing another's intent gives you the opportunity to understand what is driving them. It also gives you the opportunity, wherever and whenever it is comfortable for you, to fulfill their intent.

For example

If someone is a 'get-it-right' kind of person – for instance, your boss – making a double or triple effort to turn in high-quality work will make a major difference in your relationship with them. Letting them know that you appreciate quality work and always strive for it can have an important impact as well.

> "Joan, I've been through this document piecemeal, as I know you want it to be perfect. I'm with you on that score. I know you have a keen eye, so if you see anything that needs a quick fix, let me know. I'll be right on it."

Here you not only acknowledge who they are and what is important to them, you also let them know that it is important to you. You also let them know you have made a concerted effort to '**get it right**' and you pre-set the stage for accepting corrections and possible criticism by letting Joan know you will make every effort to fix anything that is not right. This takes away a good bit of her punch BEFORE she can pass judgment.

Communicating with Intent

Many difficult people books emphasize the communication technique of finding common ground between you and your difficult person – a place you can start from. Though your approach to life, your personality, may be different, vastly different in some cases, you can still find a place to work from. Everyone has something in common with everyone else. At the very least, it is our humanity.

Find a common ground from which you can work with them and you will find it much easier to be successful with them.

Not all or nothing

People can have more than one intent, and a different situation can bring out different intents. Each person and each situation are different.

Caution: Thinking about and working with this whole concept of 'intent' is also a form of labeling; therefore, as with any categorizing, be wise and careful in how you use it. Never discuss your 'labels' with others, and certainly never with a difficult person. Also, no one is likely to tell you their intentions outright. You will have to garner this information through skillful communication and observation.

Questions/ideas for contemplation

What is your intent when in a difficult situation with another?

Do you know what your primary motivation, 'intent,' is?

Can you figure out what the primary intent is of the difficult person/people in your life? Is it different from yours?

Chapter 18

Communications with Difficult People

Your most critical skill

Good communications skills are important in interactions with everyone and these types of skills are often emphasized in business settings. **How you communicate in difficult situations is critical to your being successful.**

[Note: We will discuss general communication skills used in difficult situations in this chapter, and then in Part III we will apply these to specific difficult behaviors.]

Listening actively

As we noted in previous chapters, many difficult people are acting difficult simply because they do not FEEL they are being heard, accepted, that they belong, and/or that their intent is getting fulfilled. **By listening carefully, attentively, and actively you can often defuse a difficult situation;** and quite possibly have a person who has been difficult in the past come to respect you because you have made the effort. Often with respect comes a change in difficult behavior.

Most of us know that listening carefully, hearing what a person is saying, is an important part of good communications. When working with difficult people, you not only need to listen carefully; you need to **let them know** you are listening to them carefully, that **they have been heard**, and that **you understand** what they are saying!

How to let them know

First, **give them a chance to talk without interruption**. Try to erase any preconceptions you have about them or what they are going to say, even if they are acting belligerently. Your calm, in-control, self-confidence will help keep the situation under control; and certainly will help defuse a situation that is out-of-control. Your willingness to let them speak first, and freely, shows respect for them and allows them to **feel** in-control. They will very likely appreciate it, and you will, at least in part, probably be filling some of their needs.

Part of listening is feedback via non-verbal communications and simple 'yeses,' 'uh-huhs,' 'nods,' etc. With difficult people you want to go beyond these important forms of feedback by being more definitive, "I hear what you are telling me," "I believe I understand what you are getting at," etc.

82

You want to go beyond even this by repeating back what they are telling you. Some authors refer to this as **backtracking**. When you repeat an important phrase, idea, bit of information back to a person, it tells them beyond any doubt that you have heard what they have said. You can go overboard with this, but most of us don't do it enough. It helps to show what you have understood; it lets them know you are really with them; and it gives you the opportunity to clarify what you have heard.

One of the keys to backtracking is to focus on important information or ideas they are saying and give them feedback on key points. Backtracking in this way is a form of acknowledgment and can be perceived as a form of recognition.

Understanding

> "...difficult people become even more difficult when they are misunderstood" (Bell and Smith)

> or perceive to be misunderstood (Koob)

Backtracking can also denote understanding and gives you the opportunity to seek clarity as well by asking follow-up questions that keep the focus on what they are telling you:

> "What I'm hearing you say is.... Does this mean that x and y are part of this?"

> "I see the connection you are making between 'A' and 'C,' so how do you see 'B' fitting into this?

Asking clarifying questions is a very useful tool for you to use to gain an understanding about something that is not clear, and an excellent way to let them know you are interested and <u>want</u> to understand.

Remember, too, that perceptions are all important. A difficult person may misunderstand what you say. Clarify whenever you feel it will help with an understanding between both of you.

Feelings

Understanding and acknowledging a person's feelings is also a key tool in communicating with difficult people. You have to say it!

> "Bob, I understand that you are very upset about this. Can you explain a bit more about X, so I have a clear picture of what you want?"

> "You seem stressed out by this, Stephanie. Will it help to go into a bit more detail, so that I can understand what needs to be done?"

> "Honey, I know you are mad at me. I'm sorry if I didn't get this right. Please help me understand what I did wrong."

Doing it with compassion and kindness is so much better.

How to ask questions

Use open-ended questions that begin with, **"how, what, when, who, where"**; avoid using "why"– it is often accusatory or seen as accusatory by someone who is overly sensitive or upset.

> "Why did you do this?"

> "Why can't you understand my side of things?"

'Why' sets a person up to be defensive.

Also, try to avoid using the word **"but,"** it qualifies and diminishes what they are telling you. A 'but' can negate all the positive in a previous statement,

> "I really like your idea, but...."

> "That's very interesting, Steve, but..."

Paying attention to what you say and how you say it when working with a difficult person can be really key to your success with them. Try to get in the habit of thinking through the verbiage you are choosing and the manner in which you present it. Someone who is upset, or someone with whom you have had previous negatively charged encounters may be ultra-sensitive to anything you say. Even statements you may feel are completely neutral may be taken the wrong way.

Take notes

This may seem odd in the middle of a difficult situation, but a simple statement like, "Hold on one second, this is obviously important to you and I want to make sure I get it right," can halt an aggressive person in their tracks. They will know that you are serious when you pull out a notebook and take notes on key points.

Seek specificity

The more you know the better. Your interest in seeking clarity, and more knowledge will often be appreciated. When you have doubts, when you are still not sure what and why this is happening **ask, ask, ask**.

Ask kindly

Bring it all together

Summarizing at the end of a conversation also **shows understanding and interest**. It lets the other person know you have been listening carefully and that you got their intent. If there are any questions on your part, or they still seem hesitant at all about what you have said, then ask them if you got it right.

Thank them

This is one of the simplest communication tools of them all, but too often we leave it out. Thank them for their input, honesty, and willingness to share. Thank them in some way. This shows compassion, caring, and a willingness to begin to bury the hatchet if your relationship has been rocky to this point.

Apologize

You may not be in the wrong, and they may be a complete jerk, but holding onto past ill will does you no good. **There are many ways to apologize without accepting blame.** Being willing to apologize helps put the ball in their court, and it can have the effect of opening the door ever-so-slightly to better communications. Once you have that opening, use your listening skills and kindness to open it further.

> "Frank, I'm sorry we have had a misunderstanding. I really think we can bury the hatchet and work together, rather than always being at odds with each other. Tell me what I need to do to make amends."

> This person is not admitting to doing anything wrong, but is willingly swallowing a little pride to change the difficult dynamics with Frank. It might be the spark that is needed to get Frank talking.

> "Elsie, I'm sorry you are so upset about the Johnson contract and the direction you feel it has taken. Can we sit down for a half hour and I'll listen carefully to what you feel is important? I think we can find a mutually agreeable solution to this concern."

> This 'apology' simply recognizes Elsie's emotions and investment in a specific concern. The apology opens the door for Elsie to have her say.

YOU have the power

By using effective listening skills and communication skills, you can offer the 'difficult' person you are dealing with a sense of power and control. The truth is, you are effectively gaining knowledge and understanding that helps you maintain a positive personal power and self-control in this situation and that will help create better interactions in the future.

Questions/ideas for contemplation

A very good exercise right now would be to take each one of the headings above and write your own thoughts and notes about them. Try to think through how you can use these key skills and tools to be an effective communicator in difficult interactions with others.

Chapter 19

Responding in Kind(ness)

Don't respond in kind – respond in kindness!

It works wonders.

Use non-verbal responses

A variety of useful tools that help show interest and understanding are always at your disposal.

Note: not all difficult people authors agree on these. I will present what I consider to be good, essential non-verbal tools.

Stance

Lean forward if you are sitting: this is a good counseling technique. It shows you are interested and 'there' with them.

If standing, stand at a comfortable speaking distance (don't get in their space or their face), stand erect, be self-confident but don't show aggression, try to be relaxed, even if the other person isn't. Mimic a stance and posture that you wish they would take.

Maintain eye contact, but without challenge.

Use nods, your eyes, and movements of your head to denote listening and understanding.

Keep hands relaxed and gesticulate without showing aggression to emphasize points.

Use silence as a tool -- allow them time to respond to you. Give respectful silence, when you feel it is needed, to allow them to collect their thoughts.

Monitor your overall demeanor. Try to show an accepting, interested, understanding, self-confident persona.

Note: some more passive types may avoid eye contact. Don't try to challenge them; look in the direction of their face and occasionally look down to indicate non-aggression.

Stay flexible

and stay alert. You may need to make adjustments by the minute to a changing and challenging situation. If you can, be flexible despite their rigidity. You will help keep the doors open for real communication and a lowering of the stakes.

87

Be patient

Be willing be to patient. It may take them several sessions to understand how you are coming across. This is especially true the first time you have your next encounter with a person you have had a difficult history with. It may take awhile for them to notice that you have changed your approach and are really making an effort to be 'with them.' You are breaking your normal script with them and their first reaction may be surprise.

Responding verbally

Let them speak first. Let them finish <u>before</u> you have your say.

Never attack. Come from a position of self-confidence and self-control. Remain calm even if they are attacking you. Never become defensive. This may be difficult, but it is critical. You have to monitor yourself carefully if you start to feel tense, angry, or upset.

If you are becoming upset, i.e. they are pushing your buttons, take deep breaths, focus on something other than what they are trying to do, which could very well be to get you to take their bait and join the fray. Focus on maintaining your **self-control**. Remind yourself that this is their stuff and you don't have to accept it or buy into it.

Ask questions, clarify, let them know what you think and feel in a calm, **self-confident** way.

Respond in a steady, clear voice that is of the same or slightly less volume than they are using. Don't try to match an angry outburst. Let it subside first. [We will talk about more specific techniques related to certain kinds of behaviors in Part III of this book.]

It is okay to disagree

Once they have had their say and you can ask, truthfully, "Is there anything else?" and you get a "No" response, then you can say what you need to say. This is important because what you have done is given them a chance to pour everything out. Now it is your turn. You have a right to stand up and have your say – kindly and positively.

Important: At difficultpeople.org we do not advocate being passive, 'giving in,' or feeling like you are being taken advantage of. We advocate coming from a **positive self-worth**, self-confident, in-control, kind, honest, and compassionate stance! You can stand up for yourself and avoid defensiveness and still be positive and kind.

> Note: Executive and personal coaches are trained in helping people learn these types of communication skills. They can be very helpful in showing someone how to be more assertive and

how to maintain their self-confidence in difficult circumstances' as well as help give many examples of HOW to say things.

Stay calm, be honest, tell them what you think and how you feel. Do it in a non-threatening way.

For example,

> "I understand that you feel this way about x. I would like you to understand how I feel."

> Or

> "I really appreciate what you have told me. I didn't know what you thought about this. Your take is very interesting. Would you like to hear my ideas on this?"

Always avoid blame

As soon as you blame someone, all the other fine work you have done comes tumbling down. Own what you say.

Own your own communication

Always use "I" statements; "you" statements are blaming. Avoid blaming at all costs. It sets the other person up to be defensive. Keep in mind that the whole point is to get beyond these difficulties.

Be brief

Brevity is the soul of wit – and it is smart tactics, too. Have your thoughts together, let them know what you think, feel, know (information), ask them if they have any questions.

Criticism

As you know, it is not uncommon for a difficult person's communications to be laced with criticism. Sometimes it is very hard to stand there calmly and listen to them rag on about you or someone else. But if you want to be successful with a difficult person, you have to remain in-control.

Listening to criticism calm, cool, and collectively takes self-confidence and self-control. Thanking them for it may be the farthest thing from what you want to do because your whole being may be screaming at you to defend yourself. **Thank them anyway.**

Thank them for their input

You don't have to agree with them about the criticism. Thank them from a neutral position.

> "I appreciate what you have said. I will consider it carefully."

> "Thanks for letting me know how you feel, Kyle. You have opened my eyes about a good many things."

Remember when responding to criticism that the tendency is to become defensive. You also have to be careful about HOW you say things. Sarcasm or any sign of negativity can destroy what you are trying to accomplish – to learn to be successful with this person's difficult behaviors.

Key point: Even unfair criticism can have some truth to it, or can tell you a good bit about what the other person is thinking, as well as the dynamics of the environment you are in – whether at work or at home

You CAN tell them – that while you appreciate their feedback, you really don't feel that it is true. Then ask them if they would like to hear your side of the story.

> "Ben, I appreciate your willingness to be open and honest with me about how you feel. I don't feel the same way, and I think you need to know that I don't really agree with some of your judgments about me. Would you be willing to listen to how I feel about all of this?"

Asking them for permission, puts them in the driver's seat from their perspective. It allows you to maintain self control and say what you need to say without sounding defensive.

Compliment them

What? This guy's trying to tear my head off!

He may be, but remember **you** are calm and collected. Complimenting a person helps to defuse a situation, and adds to a person's feelings of being accepted, acknowledged, and recognized.

Don't wait for difficult situations to arise; help them to feel better before they get difficult. Complimenting difficult people regularly, without being obsequious, is a great technique for bringing them around. There are always things you can compliment: their smile, their dress, their shoes, their work, etc. When you get a big smile, or a nice thank you, you will know you have hit the mark.

Defensiveness

Difficult people can be incredibly defensive. It is rooted in their low self-image. It can also be VERY difficult to get past. If you are dealing with a really defensive person, you will want to work very carefully on your communications, watching very carefully what you say and how you say it.

Even then it can be tough going. Positivity, kindness, and acknowledgement are absolute keys to working with defensive people. It can be a long road, too. Be patient and keep at it. If you are paying close attention, you will eventually find better ways to work with them. Perhaps the best advice I can give is – **pay them positive attention whenever you can**. When they come to respect and trust you, you will have turned a major corner.

Keep the big picture in mind

While another person is hammering at you it can be quite difficult to keep the big picture in mind.

When you really think about it, is your being <u>right</u> worth all the fuss now and the continued fuss later? Be willing to accept that someone else may not be in control, may not have everything together like you do, and may just need to get some understanding from you, not necessarily agreement.

But....

There are no "buts." "Buts" are often excuses for not doing the right or best thing.

When everything is said and done in your life

do you want it to be based on excuses?

Own your own life; don't let someone else dictate who you are by setting you up to react instead of respond.

It is unfair

Life isn't necessarily fair – at least from our somewhat limited perspectives. If you believe in a higher power, it is easy to understand that we aren't all-seeing, all-knowing, etc. Perhaps there is a good reason life is unfair to you at this moment. Perhaps that reason is for you to learn something.

Think about it.

If there is a disagreement

Ask them what they would do to resolve it. Put the ball in their court first. Listen. Understand. Then you can provide your input, after thanking

91

them for theirs. You may be surprised at how well this works, and your next interaction with this person may be quite different from what has happened between the two of you in the past.

Allow them time to respond to your ideas

Follow up your input with silence so they have time to consider what you have said and time to respond too. Encourage them to respond. Again, you are showing them courtesy and you are acknowledging them and their ideas and input further.

Negotiating

Sometimes it is tough to agree. Be open and willing to negotiate, compromise, adjust. There are almost always ways and means to bring something together. Give them plenty of leeway and stay within yourself.

Find out what they need to resolve this impasse. Then try to find a common ground from which to work from. In the process, let them know what you want and need to resolve this, too. You can propose other solutions. Keep working toward a meeting of the minds.

When you can come to the table with flexibility and a willingness to make some concessions, it is more likely that the other person will be willing to compromise on other points.

Prepare for a difficult meeting

If you know you have an encounter with a difficult person coming up, plan ahead. You can help yourself a great deal by thinking about what you want to get across, imagining how you are going to comport yourself, and practicing in front of an empty chair. Careful planning and practice help; especially until you have worked through your new skills and knowledge a few times.

It is all about Kind-frontation

Practice kind-frontation at every opportunity. Many difficult people will be affected positively by your approach. You can always find kinder ways to say things and to broach even difficult topics.

Smile

It brightens many hearts. Plus, you have just learned a tremendous amount about being successful with difficult people.

Respond in Kind(ness)

Respond WITH Kindness!

Questions/ideas for contemplation

A repeat exercise: take each one of the headings above and write your own thoughts and notes about them. Work through ideas that you have and make a list of techniques you feel might be most useful to you.

Part III

Difficult People or Difficult Behaviors?

Though we discussed the concept of difficult people in the Introduction and we further explored some aspects of difficult people in Part II, the true focal point of this book is **difficult behaviors**. The term 'difficult people' is useful because that is probably how we all think of the people in our lives that cause us angst. However, if we want to be successful in difficult encounters, we should change that focus to the difficult behaviors that people exhibit.

People, after all, are people, and it is the behavior that bothers us. Separate the negative behavior(s) from the person and you have a completely new perspective from which to build a relationship. In the next chapters we will focus on the characteristic behaviors that cause us to think of people as difficult.

Chapter 20

Negativity

Negativity is probably the one all-encompassing characteristic we can attribute to difficult behaviors. Whether the other person means to be negative or not, that is how we are seeing and experiencing their behavior. When we are in a situation with another person in which we are experiencing stress, anxiety, and perturbation, when we feel like we have been hurt by another, we are experiencing negativity.

Most people do not know they are being negative!

This is a slight, but important change, from the statement in the Introduction, "Most difficult people do not know they are being difficult."

I have known extremely negative people, and yet, they had no idea that wherever they went, with whomever they interacted, they were spreading doom and gloom.

Doom and Gloom

"The world is an awful place and there is absolutely nothing we can do about it."

"Nobody likes me; everybody hates me."

"Woe is me."

"Nothing ever good happens to me."

These are common messages that come from very negative people. For whatever reason, they just can't seem to see the positive side of things, the silver lining, in life.

Half empty

Not only do they see the glass as half empty (rather than as half full), they often can't see any way in which the glass could ever become full. Like the tendency of news agencies to focus almost exclusively on bad news, some people take everything that you and I say, do, and experience, and only seem to focus on the negative stuff.

"Nobody likes me"

A negatively centered person probably does not understand that their behavior is what pushes other people away. While they are desperate for attention and recognition, their negativity turns people off and often precludes others from even attempting to understand who they are as a person.

Doom and gloomers often see themselves as powerless to change things.

Remember when we talked about the attitude you were bringing into a difficult situation? It is very important to consider the attitude that the difficult person you are trying to deal with is bringing into the encounter. If you have had numerous concerns with this person, you probably have a good idea about what kind of attitude they have:

Depressed/Down

Frustrated

Upset/Angry

Tense

Stressed

Put upon

And so on – you can probably describe them quite well.

I have tried to emphasize a very positive, self-confident approach in this book. Regardless of the negativity someone else is bringing to the situation, you have to come in with as positive, self-confident, and in-control attitude as possible.

Negativity can really drag us down

Negatively oriented people can have a tremendous demoralizing affect on you and on anyone within their sphere of influence. Your attitude can have not only a neutralizing effect, but can also set a positive example for others; and, over time, for the difficult person you are working to be successful with.

Surprisingly, often it is not just a counter-balancing of their negativity. **People will gravitate to, and much rather be influenced by, positivity.** You can bring that very powerful force with you into any situation.

Here is a re-qualification of another statement from the Introduction:

Negativity breeds Negativity

Positivity breeds Positivity, more Positivity, and more Positivity.

It really can!

IF you stick with it!

You need to stick to your guns through rain and shine. The hard part is for you to maintain your focus and positive approach despite anything and everything the other person does or what they bring to the table.

You can make a difference

Having a very positive outlook on life and a love of sharing with others can help motivate people around you. It is attitude that affects us the most. It is the single biggest thing that you can do to help yourself, other people around you, and especially difficult people.

Don't point out their negativity

The only situation I can think of in which you can directly tell someone that they are being negative is if they specifically ask you. Even then, you want to respond as kindly as possible. **NEVER point out another person's foibles. It is blaming and produces highly defensive reactions.** You have to be patient, set a good example, and try your best to show them that there are other choices they can make.

Show them other choices

The best thing you can do is show them that there are other solutions, other choices.

In subsequent chapters we will discuss specific negatively-oriented behaviors – behaviors that make us and others very uncomfortable, angry, upset, and defensive. We will also discuss more specific ways to deal with these behaviors.

Questions/ideas for contemplation

Think of someone you know who you would characterize as negative. How would you describe their negativity?

Try making a list of characteristic ways they come across to you and others. How would you describe their behavior in detail?

When you have done this, take this list and write out how you (and others) typically respond to a given behavior or action from this person. Try to be specific. Write out your own reactions, actions, feelings, and thoughts. This exercise will help you understand the dynamics of your relationship with them and give you the knowledge to work toward being successful when you have to deal with them.

An example

"Marge is always whining and complaining about this thing or that person. It seems like general all-round negativity constantly spews from her in every direction. The whining is especially frustrating to me…well, to all of us. Some people seem to buy into her stuff and join in with the whining and finger-pointing.

"When I am around her, I quickly start to feel dragged down. It does not take long for her negativity to depress me. I do feel sorry for her. She seems so pitiable, but then I think, 'Why can't she just see a brighter side to things? Things just aren't that bad around here.'

"Generally, I try to avoid her, but I guess when I have to be in the room with her, I tend to avoid eye contact. I sit as far away as I can, and when we do make contact, I'm afraid I give her a wimpy smile, look down, and try to get away. When I finally leave her presence, I immediately feel as if a great burden has been lifted off my shoulders. It is like, 'Whew, that was intense! Now I can get on with my life.' Now that I'm paying attention to how I feel around her, I can almost see the waves of negativity flooding over me. I still want to run and hide, but I am feeling more in control and better able to handle it."

Take this exercise a step further by continuing to add to your thoughts as you work on this relationship. You will probably note dramatic changes over time.

Chapter 21

Aggressive Behaviors

Difficult behaviors take many forms and styles. In the next few chapters you will learn about some generic negative behaviors typically used by difficult people. These will be organized into three main types or categories of behaviors:

> Aggressive behaviors

> Passive-aggressive behaviors

> Passive behaviors

It is important to keep in mind that these are separately delineated for the ease of discussion. Often a single person can exhibit several types of negative behaviors. They may also change their preferred behavior(s) to another type of difficult behavior when their first choice does not work, i.e. does not get them what they want, need, or care about. There are not necessarily clear division points between different negative behaviors either.

> For example: If Bret typically gets his way by ranting and raving, but you have learned to remain calm and in-control during his tantrums, he is very likely going to try a different tack. He may try to manipulate you through behind-the-back tactics since the frontal assault isn't working any more.

A very important point to remember is that the tools and skills discussed in Part II and in the next few chapters are useful when used in a variety of difficult people situations. However, **every difficult situation is different and every difficult person is different**. You may have to try several approaches, adjust your tactics, **be flexible**, and go with the flow of the situation and the relationship.

> **Stay alert. Stay positive.**

When in doubt return to the basics:

> **Being true to yourself**

> **Remaining self-confident**

> **Maintaining self-control**

> **Practicing kindness, positivity, and compassion at every turn**

[You can always refer to *The Seven Keys to Understanding and Working with Difficult People*. (See Chapter 13.)]

98

Self-Awareness

Self-Worth

Self-Confidence

Self-Control

Honesty

Kindness

Positivity

Remember – You cannot be responsible for someone else's behavior, only your own.

Bullying

Bullies can roll over us like an out-of-control tank. They demand, dominate, push, and can be very confrontational. They are often charging ahead because they want to "get things done" (Brinkman and Kirschner), although their motivations might be varied.

Bullying is a style of behaving that has at its roots **being in control – a sense of power**. Bullies have a fear of giving over control to another and often have issues with self-worth and self-image, though they would never admit it. One of their messages is "do it my way." Another is, "I'm not interested in you or your ideas."

If you fall for their tactics and react by withdrawing or avoiding conflict (flight), or by defending yourself (fight), through confrontation, then they gain what they are after – control. Yet, **if you maintain your self-control, their 'out-of-control' behavior loses any possibility of gaining what they want from you.**

The message you want to send

The hardest thing when confronted by an overwhelming, attacking force is to remain calm and in complete control. Everything in your body wants to react to protect yourself. However, **the most important message to send to a bully is that their tactics have no effect on you**. The best way to do that is to **stand assertively**, but not confrontationally, and **maintain your poise** no matter what. Be with your thoughts and emotions, but don't give-in to them. Let them talk and let their outburst wind down – which will happen IF you don't react. If you fight back, escalation of the confrontation is inevitable and the sky is the limit thereafter.

Listen and learn

The communication techniques discussed in Part II of this book are paramount. You want to let them know that you will pay attention to them and what is important to them, but only from a calm and in-control stance. **Listen actively** -- show that you are listening by giving positive non-verbal and verbal cues; let them know you are listening by backtracking; and indicate understanding by asking questions, rephrasing what they have said, and by **giving them positive feedback**.

Be patient, be attentive, wait until the power and tension has dissipated, and then tell them that you appreciate their thoughts. Summarize what they have been talking about and then feel free to ask them whether they would be willing to listen to your ideas. Do this with a calm, but firm intonation (you are in control of you!). Be willing at any point to listen to them if they have something else to say.

If they 'start in' again, they may have missed the point that their tactics aren't working with you, so you will need to let them have their say once more and let them wind down.

Stay within yourself, stay patient, eventually they will run out of steam and they will see that you have no intention of getting into a confrontation with them. It is even possible that they may calm down and listen carefully to what you have to say.

Keep in mind that facial expressions, body language, etc. all send messages. Try to stay calm and non-committal. Reacting in any way may exacerbate the encounter.

Tell them how you feel

At some point, if you feel it is appropriate and they are willing to listen, say something like,

> "I'm always willing to listen to your ideas and concerns, John. Just for future reference, I would sincerely appreciate a kinder, gentler approach. You know I am here for you."

You have a right not to be bullied!

Key point: Bullies lose all their steam when they can't get you to react. Then there is a good chance that they will look at you in an entirely different way from that point on. Your relational dynamics with them will have changed dramatically. They may begin to respect you and your ideas, and this can be the start of a completely new type of relationship with this person.

Exploding behavior

Bullies can be pretty intense. There is, in essence, another form of bullying that takes on a slightly different approach – the difficult person who just suddenly explodes, and sometimes you have absolutely no idea why, can present some additional difficulties.

Everything mentioned above about dealing with bullies is appropriate in working with this exploding-type as well, however, there are several other important considerations.

Getting a person who is ranting and raving to calm down, may take another tactic. A good skill to learn is to just keep saying the person's name over and over again, until they stop and pay attention to you.

"Alan…Alan…Alan…Al…I'm here Al; Talk to me…"

Once they stop, you have the opportunity to say something akin to, "Alan, I'm listening. Please calm down and we will get to the bottom of this." [Note: this can also work with strangers. Just repeat 'Sir,' or Ma'am' until they calm down.]

They may not know either

It is sometimes quite difficult to know what is motivating the exploder, i.e. what 'sets them off.' Often, they don't even know themselves. It may be their way of gaining attention; or it may simply be a build up of tension and stress from other sources throughout their day, and you just happen to be in the way at the wrong time. Or, this could be the way they have always gotten others to do what they want. Remember, all difficult people gain something from their behavior.

Don't give it to them…directly

Don't fall into their traps.

Very important: As with any difficult person, you want to understand what they need, want, care about and give them that, if possible; but by positive means and NOT by reinforcing their negative behavior.

In any case, your tactics remain the same. They need help in getting under control, and **you can assist them with that because you are in control** and have the patience and communication skills to help them.

Try to view the person who tends to explode compassionately. They are obviously getting their buttons pushed in some way or they are pushing their own buttons. You can be the person who brings the totally opposite dynamic to the situation. By paying attention, understanding, and being compassionate, it is very likely you will fill their needs in a kind-frontational way instead of a confrontational way.

Obnoxious, rude, and boorish

Some difficult people exhibit some very obnoxious behaviors. Their approach is not necessarily that of a bully or an exploding personality, but they manage to come across as extremely negative people. They can use offensive language, tell inappropriate jokes and stories, or just generally rag on you and other people.

Though the task may be noxious and difficult, the same tactics as used with other aggressive personalities work with them. Pay no heed to the difficult behavior, work with them to understand what they want and need (usually attention). Give it to them through your constantly improving communication skills. Then, when the time is right, let them know that you would prefer they approach you in a kinder, less volatile, and nicer way.

Be yourself

Be positive

Be kind

Surprise, surprise, surprise! (Are you old enough to remember Gomer Pyle?)

These tactics can and do work. Try them.

Take care: **WARNING!**

Only you can truly understand the difficult people and difficult situations you find yourself in. Unless you are working closely with a coach, you are out there on your own. If you have any sense that the person you are dealing with is under the influence of alcohol, drugs and/or has significant mental problems, LEAVE the situation immediately and get help. If this is a person you regularly encounter, please get help, for your sake, your-coworkers' sake, and for them. Use the appropriate legal and administrative venues at your place of employment to work through this difficult situation. Please never put yourself or anyone else at risk.

When in doubt, be safe

Though the tactics and skills presented in this book may help in working with a person who has serious concerns, it is far better to be safe, than sorry.

Questions/ideas for contemplation

Now is the time for practical application: try putting all the things you have learned into field practice. You won't have to look for difficult situations – we get enough of them as it is. But when you find yourself in one, start

102

using these skills and techniques. Mental practice ahead of time (in front of a mirror, or even with a friend or coach) can be very valuable.

You may want to practice your self-awareness skills, as well as pay attention to your self-worth, self-confidence, positivity, and kindness when dealing with others before working this magic with a difficult person in your life.

At first, you may make some mistakes and you may find yourself feeling awkward. Practice will definitely help. Stick with your self-development program and you will make a difference. If you feel you need help, consider hiring a personal coach for a brief period. They will help you work on your skills and techniques.

Chapter 22

Aggressive Behaviors II

Button pushers

While bullies, exploders, and generally obnoxious people can push our buttons, there are aggressive types who use 'putting-down' behavior as their method of choice (which is also sometimes found in bullies, exploders, and other obnoxious, rude, and boorish folks).

Criticism and sarcasm: 'putting-down' behavior

Putting down other people is a way difficult people boost themselves up. It is how many difficult people feed their egos. It is probably the most common 'button-pushing' behavior there is.

> Author's Note: I knew a very difficult person who seemed to always need to have a person on his 'hit list' to deprecate and put-down. In the course of time that I knew this person, he always had someone to denigrate and when he latched on to someone, he didn't let go. When that person either left because he/she was tired of the treatment, or was fired because this guy managed to convince the boss that he was terrible at what he did, this guy immediately picked another person to step on. It seemed like he couldn't exist within the parameters of the workplace without having someone he could put down to raise himself up.

Sadly, he saw himself as a positive, outgoing, highly religious person. He had no clue as to how he came across to others. He is one of the most obnoxious and difficult people I have ever met or worked with. Even his friends shook their heads at his tactics and behaviors.

Is there anything you can do?

Some putting-down behavior is direct, in our face. This we can usually deal with directly. However, some of it, often a good bit of it, is behind our backs. (We will talk about backstabbing behavior in the passive-aggressive section.)

You can work with direct 'put-down' behavior directly.

Responding positively and **remaining in control** when someone is deprecating you and your work is tough, but, as with other direct, in our face, aggressive behaviors, it is the only behavior that will work successfully.

Use your communication skills, because this person needs to be heard and you need to give them time to be heard. Only after they have had their say, completely, with you using your skills to draw out all they need to say to you, can you respond. A good communication technique to use with criticizers is to **seek clarification of what they mean**, what they **want, what is motivating them**. Then you have to thank them.

Thank them?

Yup – thank them for their feedback.

You don't have to agree with it, but you don't want to defend yourself, no matter how much you want to – at least not directly or confrontationally. **Defense is seen by others as offense**, and it will invariably raise the stakes of the encounter and exacerbate the situation.

Thank them for being open and honest about how they feel; then ask them if you could give them your side of the story. Then tell them. Provide them with ideas, facts, understandings they may not have considered or known about.

Do this calmly and with their permission. Try to make it seem like they hold all the keys. Keep in the back of your mind that **power and control are often side issues in these types of situations**. As long as you are in control of you, you can afford to let them feel in control of the situation.

Once you have been able to say what you think and have been able to share your ideas, be open to further comments and ideas from them. **Try to establish a dialogue, a common ground, instead of a conflict.** Pause often to let them have their say. Don't be surprised if it takes a little while for them to move off their 'high and mighty' platform and come down to talk with you as a mere mortal. Be patient and stay with the conversation.

Always come from a position that shows you are interested in their feedback and their ideas.

> "I appreciate that, Alice, I will definitely think about that."

> "Thanks, Bob, I will take that into consideration…"

> And so on.

Tell them how you feel

It is important to let them know how you feel about their approach at some point. "Carl, I really appreciate this feedback, but it was rather upsetting the way you said it. Could we just sit down and talk the next time? I am always ready to listen to what you have to say.

Keep in mind

This is a learned behavior. They have had lots of practice. Change takes time and they will not likely learn this in one or two sessions. You need to be patient and give them a chance to understand that you are approaching things differently with them, and that you don't intend to accept their negativity anymore. You may have to work through this strategy a number of times before they get it.

NOTE: Just letting people talk and have their say is a remarkable thing. Often, it can be the start of a change in dynamics between you and another person. It might not work either; but it is worth a try. Negativity just isn't worth it.

Also, remember that **positivity** is the great equalizer and beyond! It is tough for someone to maintain negativity in the face of persistent positivity

Blaming

Blaming is, in essence, a form of criticism or put-down behavior. It is also a very common button pusher. All the tactics discussed above should be used with inveterate blamers. You don't have to accept their blame, but it is useful to listen to what they have to say. You can find out a good bit about who they are and who you are in the process. **Be understanding** and learn all that you can, before emphasizing through your own responses that you are an assertive, kind, self-confident, in-control person who is willing to stand up for yourself, **positively**.

(We will also talk about this more under passive-aggressive behaviors, as blaming often includes third-party tactics.)

Just don't let them push your buttons!

Blame can really raise our hackles. Resist the impulse to defend yourself. "I did not!" is a natural reaction/response, but it does not do any good with blamers. Until you are willing to listen, pay attention, understand what they want to get across, and then work with their needs, it won't do any good to state your case.

Be patient and get your words in, not edgewise, but when they feel satisfied that you understand them and where they are coming from. You can gently let them know that you would prefer they come and ask you, personally, if further concerns arise, and that you will be happy to hear them out at any time.

Once they have had their say, their full say, then you can discuss your ideas, feelings, and you may even be able to disagree with them. Disagree politely and kindly. There are always kind ways to say things

Power and Greed

Power and Greed are powerful motivators and can be at the root of difficult aggressive and even passive-aggressive behaviors. Usually these are deeply rooted in fear. It is very important to remember that in spite of all you do, that people who are extremely motivated will find other ways to get what they want.'

People who are motivated by power and/or greed tend to be willing to push all others aside (in various negative ways) to get what they want. Sometimes you have to decide if it is worth the trouble to be around such people.

We discuss people who exhibit strongly motivated and frequent difficult behaviors (really difficult people!) near the end of this book.

Word of caution: sometimes negative people, blamers, the power hungry, etc. manage to influence others to take up their banner or come on board their methods. Stick to your positivity guns; you never have to buy into their behaviors.

Aggressive behaviors

Aggressive people are typically in our face because they are so out-in-the-open. If we can remain in control of ourselves and of our own positive approach, we can deal with these behaviors successfully. As you will see passive-aggressive and passive behaviors are not necessarily as easy to respond to.

Questions/ideas for contemplation

Think of a situation in which you have been criticized, put down, blamed (or imagine such a situation). Can you stay calm and focused? Can you maintain your self-worth and self-confidence? Can you imagine using some of your communication skills and using the approach above successfully?

If you regularly have to deal with this type of difficult behavior, this form of mental and emotional practice can be invaluable.

Chapter 23

Passive-aggressive Behaviors

Generally speaking, passive-aggressive behavior is behavior that is not 'in your face' aggressive, but is aggressive indirectly.

Passive-aggressive behaviors include complaining about you behind your back (backstabbing), whining, gossiping, lying, acting like they know it all, etc. People who exhibit these behaviors can be just as difficult, and in some cases more difficult, than openly aggressive types, and they can cause you just as much angst!

"I'm Perfect"

Perfectionists, know-it-alls, act-like-they-know-it-alls, blamers, and nit-pickers can be very frustrating to us mere mortals. In the presence of a person who exhibits these behaviors, we feel like we can do nothing right. It actually seems like they really do feel like we can do nothing right. We feel as if **we are not good enough**.

The sad and, perhaps, surprising thing is that they don't feel this way at all. They usually have a very low self-image. THEY feel that they are not good enough. Their behavior is a cry for help; an attempt to be so perfect that no one can find fault with them. In some cases, like the aggressive put-er-downers and criticizers, it is also the way that they elevate themselves – by putting others in their place.

"Just the facts, ma'am" (Apologies to **Dragnet**)

The perfectionist comes from what they consider to be a very factual, pragmatic, practical viewpoint. They don't see their behavior as negative, and usually have little or no understanding about how they frustrate others. They feel like they are simply reporting or responding to the facts.

Here is a perspective on perfectionist behavior:

Let's say my team and I turn in a report that states,

"The tigers need to be <u>watchd,</u> they can be very dangerous."

The perfectionist may read this and react like we have really screwed up. Subtle or not, they WILL let us know that we made a mistake. Even if this is the only mistake in a hundred-page report, they will find it and remark on it in some way. They will be sure to let you know that you screwed up.

This can be a very passive reaction on their part: a look of disbelief, a terse memo stating that we need to proofread our work or else, a 'down their nose look at us' at the next board meeting, etc. Whatever form they use to indicate their displeasure, you will get the hint. Subtle or not, they get the point across that you are not good enough.

They literally react as if we had written: "The tigers are friendly, they need to be petted."

From our perspective, they are over-reacting. Not so much because they found a mistake in our report and drew our attention to it, but because of how we typically feel about the way they let us know about it. Their manner makes us feel less-than, not-good-enough, blamed, etc.

Pointing out minor faults and foibles is the 'game' of the perfectionist or nit-picker. To the receiver, it is anything but a game. While the perfectionist may think they are only pointing something out, 'so we can do better next time,' or improve to their standards, we are likely to feel as if we've been hit in the stomach. Partly, this is because of their manner, and partly, because it is their modus operandi – it is how they do business day in and day out. You probably wouldn't think twice about it if it only happened occasionally:

> You are wrong; they are right.

> You make mistakes; they don't ever seem to make any (at least from their perspective).

> They always point out yours and others' mistakes; you tend to let things go by without comment because they are not worth fussing about most of the time.

Nitpickers seem to have an almost uncontrollable need to point out when we haven't done something the way they would have done it, e.g. an occasional rare mistake in our work, leaving a drawer open, dropping a sock on the way to the laundry, not saying what they expect us to say, and so on. It almost seems like we can do nothing right.

It seems like they are always "pissed off" at us. We just aren't **good enough**.

They just don't seem to understand that the world would be so much kinder, gentler, more peaceful and beautiful, not to mention have a whole lot less tension in it, if they said things in kinder ways, or were willing to ignore occasional mistakes or fix it themselves. It would be nice if they could find ways of dealing with people other than blaming, complaining, and pointing out their mistakes or lapses in judgment.

How can we show them?

First: be the best possible example; be the best you can be.

This is the place to start, but there is more you can do. Remember, we discussed trying to fulfill a difficult people's needs, wants, cares, intent? Ask yourself, "What does this person need? What do they care about? What do they really want?"

Generally, perfectionists want to be accepted. They can gobble up all the support, attention, and acceptance we can throw at them and more. Patience and kindness can work with these difficult people.

Pay them positive attention on a regular basis and their need to point out yours and other's foibles may dissipate somewhat. It probably won't completely go away, it is too fundamental to who they are. They have used it successfully for far too long; still, you can make a significant difference.

Another technique you could try is thanking them. This is the opposite reaction to what they expect. Let them know you are trying to work on your 'problem.' Try to couple this with sincere kindness.

> "Thanks for pointing that out to me, Stan, I appreciate it. I am really working on doing better, but you know keeping things organized is not my strong point. Thanks for staying on top of things"

You can also make an effort to live up to their standards, which may help ameliorate them to a certain extent; but you may as well face the truth – you will never succeed; you will never be good enough for them.

Keep in mind that most of the time they don't see their behavior as derogatory.

Ultimately, we have to accept who we are and how we do things and learn to not be so affected by their approach to us and to life. IMPORTANT: **This is their stuff, not ours. We know we are good enough.**

Most importantly,

Don't react negatively to their nitpicking

They probably expect a reaction. Consciously or subconsciously they know you will get upset, fire a salvo back at them, feel bad, etc. The result will be that they feel in control, they feel power, they feel better about themselves, and they have gotten some of the attention they need.

Your best tactic in many cases is to smile and ignore what they are trying to get you to react to.

Say,

> "Thanks"

> "Got it"

"Makes sense"

Anything that is positive or neutral and non-committal.

IMPORTANT!

Trust me, this is not easy to do when you are dealing with someone who seems to need to point out all your mistakes, foibles, etc. With such a person, you may just ultimately need to sit down with them and tell them how you feel about their approach, how it hurts you, and ask them kindly to adjust the way they deal with you on a regular basis. They very well may not have a clue how they are coming across. This is one of those situations where this type of negative behavior seems to be based in a very low self-image. AND/OR it is just how they were treated by someone in their life, and it is essentially a learned behavior.

Make sure that you stay on top of your own feelings. Perfectionists can get to us – we need to maintain our positivity in spite of their pickiness.

Replace their negativity with positive self-enhancing statements:

> "I am good enough."

> "Ignore that; you have done a great job on this and you know it."

> And so on.

With a perfectionist around, it is also helpful to form an informal support group of people who also have to deal with this person. IMPORTANT! This is not a gripe group. The purpose should be to encourage and support each other, not to complain, whine, and put someone down. Positivity breeds Positivity; Negativity breeds Negativity.

They won't/don't get it

Don't try to convince the perfectionist that what they are picking at isn't important. You can argue 'til you are blue in the face' and they won't 'get it.' Remember the discussion of Classic versus Romantic? Perfectionists tend to be those who love everything in 'neat little piles.' They truly find it very difficult to understand those of us who are of the opposite persuasion.

Help them be better critics

Sometimes the opposite strategy works: "if you can't lick 'em, join 'em."

At work you could make them an official or unofficial quality control specialist. Outside of work, let them know that you want all the help you can get from them pointing out your foibles.

"Thanks, Darlene. I needed that. Would you mind paying some extra attention to my work in the future. I really want to be the best I can be, and you have such a keen eye, it would be helpful if I want to advance to the next level to make sure everything is top notch."

Chances are they will get tired of the 'game' when you are playing along with them. It is just not fun anymore and it does not give them what they need – reinforcement. Darlene probably won't want to help you get ahead, either. Plus, when you take this stance, their tactics don't seem to carry the heavy weight or negative charge that they have before. Somehow asking them to be picky helps you be more in control of you

The best strategy

Is to be yourself – your best in-control, self-confident, positive self. Being successful with this type of difficult people does not necessarily take honing your communication skills, but it does take rising above the nit-picking and believing in your own self-worth.

Don't let another person determine your self-worth!

Smile, accept, be gracious, understand that they are doing this because of THEIR issues, not yours.

Questions/ideas for contemplation

Have a nit-picker/perfectionist in your life? Try a few of the strategies discussed above during the week. See what kind of response you get. See how you feel as a result. Try this for several weeks and see if the overall dynamics change with this person.

Be sure to avoid any hint of negativity, sarcasm, or blame. Stay in-control and be positive.

Step back and see if you can maintain a positive attitude when you are being 'picked on.' Watch what happens when you don't react negatively to what they have said. How do they react when you stay calm and in-control?

Chapter 24

Passive-Aggressive Behaviors II

Complaining, Whining, Gossiping

These doom and gloomers seem to exude negativity. They can't seem to find anything positive to say about others or the world in general. There is always something wrong.

Their motivation isn't necessarily to 'get' anyone in particular, but to let the world know how terrible they feel. How depressing everything is.

The most important perspective you can bring to this type of behavior is that it is very detrimental in the long run. At work, at home, and in social settings, **complainers, whiners, and gossipers undermine everyone's positivity and self-worth**.

What can you do?

First, maintain your positivity. Positivity, if you and others stick to your guns, will trump negativity. You have to be determined to spread the opposite of what this person tends to spread. Support, encourage, appreciate, recognize and reward everyone – yes, even the doom and gloomer. Get others on the same bandwagon.

Getting others on-board

When working with pervasively negative people, one key idea to always keep in mind is **being willing to get help** -- help from colleagues, or friends, or family members depending on the situation. This means actually talking with others about getting on board with your positivity campaign, and using skills and ideas such as appreciation, recognition, positive contact, and so on. The more the merrier – literally!

Tactics

Doom and gloom spreaders need to become involved; **they need to feel wanted and accepted**. Spend only a brief time, if any, listening to their complaints and then follow up with any of the following approaches:

For complainers

> "I appreciate what you are saying, and I commiserate with your concerns; however, let's see if we can work on some ideas to help solve this problem."

Be solution oriented

If at all possible, get them on track and motivated to do something about what they are complaining about. If they are an inveterate complainer, this may not work. But they will probably stop complaining around you, because you won't play their game of doom and gloom and finger-pointing.

Start a complaint contract

If you are the boss (or you could suggest this to your boss to have him/her implement it), let the complainer and everyone else in your organization know that when they have a complaint they need to fill out a form and write at least three or four possible approaches for a solution at the bottom. Any complaint with no solution costs a buck. Or they can state the complaint, but need to follow it up quickly (set a time limit) with some possible solutions. [Note: This can also work at home.]

You might be surprised at how quickly people get into the swing of things and will gleefully point out to others that they just said something that sounded like a complaint without solutions attached and they need to 'feed the kitty.'

Use the money for a party at the end of the quarter/year.

> Author's Note: Here is a related tactic I used with my kids for putting their seat belts on years ago.
>
> We instigated a rule that anyone who didn't have their seatbelt on got an incessant patting on the top of their head until they accomplished the task. Guess who ended up with the most pats on the head? Good ol' Dad! They learned VERY quickly.

For whiners

Again, you can listen briefly, but don't get dragged into the 'woe is me' and 'woe is the world' syndrome. Instead, "kill them with kindness." (Brinkman and Kirschner)

Whiners are looking for attention. Your choice is to buy into the 'woe' they are delivering, or to give them attention through a much more positive approach. Spending even brief periods of positive, supportive time on a regular basis with whiners can help improve their outlook, increase their productivity, and help you build a strong interactive relationship with them.

Getting other positive people to join you in spreading kindness to the inveterate whiner can be a great help too.

Gossipers

Gossipers can be the most detrimental people in an organization. We all gossip sometimes, but for some people it seems to be a mission. They can easily destroy a work or group environment if they are allowed to go unchecked. Never allow gossiping to be tolerated. Deal with it with kind-frontation skills and by **bringing everything out in the open**. It is hard to gossip about something that everyone knows about.

Gossipers are also looking for attention, but they may not respond as well to kindness and as readily to paying them positive attention as the whiner. Gossipers usually have been at their game too long. However, positivity is always worthwhile. Remember it tends to rub off on everyone.

Sometimes you just have to let them know

Complainers, whiners, gossipers, and blamers, especially gossipers, need to know that their behavior is detrimental and unacceptable. You may just have to tell them as kindly and honestly as possible:

> "Bob, I don't like to gossip (blame, complain, whine) about others. If you have a concern with Betty, why don't you talk with her directly."

Or,

> "I really appreciate what you are telling me about so and so. She is just down the hall. Let's go down there and discuss this together."

Whoa!

This will typically stop them right in their tracks. They REALLY don't want to have this discussion with so-and-so. If you do this several times, they will get the idea that you have a no-nonsense approach to complaining, whining, gossiping, and blaming about others.

You can also make office/house/organizational guidelines. Brainstorm positive ways to get people on track so that these behaviors don't get rewarded and positive behaviors do. (See the 'complaint contract' above.) There are many similar ideas that can be implemented. Bring everyone together to brainstorm; then they will get the message that this behavior is not to be tolerated and that they can be part of the solution.

Again! **Helping difficult people be part of a solution is often a great strategy. Then they own part of their own improvement plan**

Backstabbing, lying, undermining behavior

Complainers, blamers, gossipers can all be detrimental to your peace and the peace and functioning of your organization and your home life. They can undermine your success and your team's success. Backstabbers/liars are the worst of the lot. They can undermine your credibility and the credibility of your department, organization, etc. They can even get people (you) fired.

Backstabbers, et al, have a very low self-image; they have a great need for acceptance, and they may also have a very strong need or drive for greed and/or power. They can be very dangerous!

These types need to be approached cautiously and carefully. They may have a network and have a good bit more influence than you think.

In working with this behavior, all your communications skills are critical. Maintaining your cool is even more critical. The keys are:

> **Getting things out in the open** – when it is 'out there,' they can't use it for ammo

> **Being open and honest about who you are** and what you do, as well as **what you are willing to accept**

> Insist on others being open and honest with you

> Be willing to kind-front them about their behind-the-back tactics

At some point you need to let them know you know.

Backstabbers and liars will probably not stop their behavior unless you kind-front them with it. You don't have to attack them or put them on the defensive. Own your own communications: use 'I' statements whenever possible, avoid 'You' statements. Give them a chance to explain.

> "John, I understand that you may have said something about my not putting in any time on the Cherney project. You know that I did most of the work on that project. Can we discuss this? I want to hear your side of the story."

Listen to what they say (they will invariably deny it) and then respond with something like,

> "Thanks, I appreciate your clearing that up. However, if you do have any problems with what I do, I would appreciate your coming directly to me in the future." Be firm, but don't challenge them, even if you know they are lying. Your purpose is solely to let them know you are on top of things.

Stay on top of things!

If they come back with, "Who told you I said that?" **Don't tell them.** If the person who told you is a close friend and confidant, who is looking out for your best interests, you need to protect them. If the informant is a possible gossip/liar/backstabber themselves, then you need to gather as much information as possible.

Keep your ear to the ground. Gather as many facts as you can. Stay close to them. Backstabbers won't stop with one response/rebuttal from you. You have to let them know you are on to their negative tactics. You will have to kind-front them several times, at least.

Keep a log and documentation. You cannot be too careful; they may go even further underground.

Continue to be a positive force

Your greatest weapon with the liar and backstabber is your true self. **Make sure that others** (coworkers, employees, your boss) **see who you truly are and what kind of work you do.** Let them know that what they have heard is not true and that you are upset that someone would spread such rumors.

Tell them

It is okay, it is important, to let them know that lying is not acceptable and you won't put up with it. You can do it kindly but firmly.

> "John, I want you to know I believe in total honesty between all of us here at work. I hope you will be honest with me, as I feel it is very important to our relationship."

In certain situations, you may be able to bring others into the picture to kind-front the backstabber or liar. If other people are willing, a meeting with them, the difficult person, and your boss, might be appropriate and needed. Let the difficult person know that their behavior has been noticed, that it is unacceptable, and that only positive behavior will be rewarded. Be as positive as possible, but be firm.

Questions/ideas for contemplation

Complainers, whiners, gossipers, backstabbers, liars, cheats – difficult people! Try writing one strategy each week for dealing with each of these 'types.' What would a successful strategy for working with them look like? How would you approach them? What would you say? Plan carefully, remain positive.

Chapter 25

Passive Behaviors

I'm not quite convinced that there really is such a thing as passive behavior. It seems like an oxymoron. Behavior connotes action. However, in the parlance of psychology and the difficult people literature, there are a number of behaviors that are defined as being significantly passive.

Unlike aggressive and passive-aggressive personalities, where the person's behavior is either directly or indirectly affecting you, passive behavior tends to frustrate us because little or nothing is happening. **It is the lack of response that can produce difficult situations.**

More than anywhere else, unresponsive people can be a thorn in the side of a business team.

Unresponsive behavior

As a broad category, the passive personality is generally unresponsive. To an active, motivated person whose aim is to get things accomplished and move ahead, the unresponsive person can be extremely frustrating.

The need of an unresponsive person is to "get along." (Brinkman and Kirschner) They are often fearful of making mistakes, disappointing people, and they avoid conflict at all costs. Their typical response to any stress is avoidance (flight).

To be successful with them you have to make an effort to bring them back into the fold. Help them to become interested, active, and participating in life and work again. The key is to **make it safe for them to become involved**. Let them experience safely making choices themselves.

Do nothing behavior/slacking off

Sometimes nothing can be more frustrating than a coworker, employee, boss who does the bare minimum to survive. You want to engage them, get them going, and help them to be productive, but nothing seems to work. To make it even more frustrating, they often will not seem willing to communicate with you either.

Patience

When working with the do-nothing/unresponsive person the most important thing is to remember that **their behavior is rooted in fear**. They may be paralyzed in a sense because they are afraid of any kind of conflict

– they just want to get along. They are afraid that doing something, anything, may create a problem, and/or they may have a morbid fear of making mistakes.

Be patient. Any sign of frustration on your part will drive them deeper into their shell.

Be extra kind and friendly

Engaging an unresponsive, do-nothing personality takes patience and kindness. It also takes time and daily effort. Let them see you as a **supportive, friendly, caring person**. Go out of your way for awhile to help them and support them whenever it is feasible.

Communicate with them regularly to draw them out. Start with open-ended questions about everything except what you want and need. Discuss their interests, family, the weather, anything that might get them to begin to open up. You may be doing 99% of the talking to start with. Give them lots of time to respond, especially if they are not responding at all. Act like you are expecting a response. Goad them if necessary:

> "Can you tell me what you think about what I just said?"

> "So how do you feel about this?"

> "Do you have an opinion about…?"

Help them feel needed

Getting them involved and more active may simply be letting them know that they are valuable, that their input and skills are needed, and that they understand where and how they fit into the process of the team's development. Give them plenty of information, feedback, and support about their importance in the process.

Ask them:

> What they need to feel safe and comfortable

> What they want to be able to do their job well

> What they care about

> What would really help them to feel good (their needs/desires)

If they respond, then follow-up by exploring a variety of possibilities with them. You may be able to get them engaged in the process of making this situation safe and amenable to their needs.

Ask them what would make the most difference in their work/life. Even if it is pie-in-the-sky, it is a starting point for further exploration.

Get them started...

If it is within your purview, help them be empowered by assigning easy, short tasks that they can be 100% successful with. If you have been able to draw them out a bit, use the information you have garnered to tailor their involvement in tasks at work to their interests and expertise. Praise and support them frequently.

Give them the opportunity to be part of the whole process of designing their involvement. **Get them involved and focused on solutions.** Keep the process and solutions manageable and short-term to start with. Make sure they are successful at every turn.

As they develop more and more confidence, ask them if they want more responsibility. See if they want to be more involved. Play to their strengths, especially if they are different from your strengths.

Never criticize

Passive personalities are often extremely sensitive to any type of criticism. Find ways to **couch things in positive ways**. Try to offer support and encouragement when things don't go well for them. Help them get back on their feet.

If you have the opportunity, bring other people into the mix and get them to offer support and encouragement, too.

The payoff is that you may make a very unproductive, seemingly sullen person an active and valuable member of your team (work) or a more engaged person (at home/socially). The BIG payoff is you can feel good about helping someone get enervated by life again.

Procrastinating

Some people just can't seem to get finished. They may have trouble making decisions, which often comes from a fear of failure, a fear of making mistakes.

As with the unresponsive, do-nothing personality, the key is to make it safe for them to get things done. Use the tools discussed above, and keep in mind that one of the keys is to **break tasks into small manageable pieces** so they can be highly successful. Eventually, you will need to train them to do this themselves. This will help save you time and effort.

Involving them in the planning process of moving from point A to point B can also give them a better perspective on how to get the job done and completed and show them how important their piece is to the overall picture.

Make sure they are on the right seat on the bus

It is not uncommon for a person to be completely unmotivated because they feel out of place. If they are in a job they hate, or working with someone who drives them crazy, it might be wise to help them find another niche. You probably won't find out what turns them on, unless you are willing to ask.

A great mentoring skill that we sometimes forget to use is to **get people talking about what would really make a difference in their life**. While they may say, "To win the lottery," if you get them talking, you will find out what they ARE interested in. Very few people just want to laze around in life and contribute nothing. While it may not be your responsibility, helping them light their own personal fire, may help make your life easier – it might be worth the effort.

Make it safe for them to make mistakes

People can freeze up because they are afraid to finish. Perfectionists can fit into this category – the need to have everything right, precludes anything ever making it off their desk. **Create an environment where creativity, flexibility, and innovation are rewarded.** If the environment is comfortable and safe to create in, they will notice, and generally will get swept up in the process. Just be willing to give them time to feel safe and to get involved.

"Yes" or over-committing behavior

The "I will do that" person volunteers for everything. They take on task after task and everyone enthusiastically dumps whatever they don't want to do in their laps. Unfortunately, they will all soon discover that none of it ever gets done. The 'Yes' person is desperate to accommodate everyone; they typically take on much more than they are capable of handling. They need to be accepted and to get along with everyone.

Task management skills are critical: keeping on top of what their workload is and how they are moving through a given task are both important. This can take some time, but you are helping to train them in the process. Encourage them as they successfully complete different tasks. As their confidence builds, your hands-on, time commitment will lessen and you may just come out of this with a very valuable employee or coworker.

As usual your communications skills and people skills can bring a tremendous amount to the situation.

Be kind

Keep it positive

Pay attention to them

Encourage/support

Acknowledge them – frequently

Appreciate who they are and what they do accomplish

Recognize and Reward even small accomplishments to start with

Keep in mind...

that passive behavior requires a consistent positive approach. Any hint of negativity or judgment will have them scurrying back to their hiding place. If you are frustrated with them, they will notice.

> Practice gentle kindness. Become a seemingly omni-present positive, supportive force in their lives. Give them a chance and they will blossom.

Questions/ideas for contemplation

Do you know any unresponsive people? Can you imagine working through the ideas above to establish a positive outcome with this person over a period of time? Detailing a plan to work with passive personalities is a good strategy.

Working to bring a passive person out of their shell can be taxing and frustrating because what you wish you could do is shout, "Come on get with the program!" You can't, so be sure to stay on top of how you are feeling and remember to take care of yourself. **Gentleness** is a good word to keep in mind when working with passive personalities.

Chapter 26

Different People/Different Approaches

We have only indirectly discussed how people in different circumstances and in different relationships affect their interactions with each other. How you interrelate with someone at work (or socially) can determine what type of approach you choose and the skills and tools you can use to be successful with them. For example:

Spouses

Coworker to Coworker

Boss to Employee

Employee to Boss

Customer Service Representative to Customer

And so on.

In this chapter we will focus on some of the typical people you interact with on a daily basis. This will be a brief overview of how some of these differences in relationships can affect your general approach and how different people can affect the choices you make in how you respond in a given situation.

> Note: Many of the other book titles available at our website focus specifically on a wide variety of relationships we have in work and in life. [See Appendix III for an annotated listing of Dr. Koob's books available at Amazon.com.]

Difficult Bosses

Tread lightly, but always remember you have choices and you have the right not to be bullied. Staying calm, cool, and collected is essential, as you might imagine. **Power and Control** are key factors in working with a difficult boss. Understanding how to address issues is important to your survival.

Information is one of the keys to working with difficult bosses. Find out their needs, wants, and concerns. **Communicate wisely and frequently, and provide them with updates of what you are doing and accomplishing**.

The next chapter will be on writing skills. **Keep your boss on top of who, what, where, when, how, and why IN WRITING. This creates a valuable paper trail and also keeps her/him informed.** Information can

123

help keep difficult bosses happier with you and what you are trying to accomplish.

Key point: **bosses like to be informed BRIEFLY**. Keep it short

Difficult Coworkers

Keep in mind that these are the people you spend most of your time with. A good working relationship is critical. You can be the catalyst for positive relations with them.

Competition is also very common in the work place. Letting a fellow coworker know that you don't want to be in constant competition with them can help ease some tension. **Staying positive and doing your own work well to the best of your ability is the best approach to competition.**

Difficult Employees

Much of what has been detailed in previous chapters gives you key skills and ideas to use with difficult employees. Remember that YOUR approach and style will have a tremendous effect. Building your own positive, approachable, flexible managing persona can be extremely effective in dealing with difficult employees.

Being an effective manager of people is called leadership. **Leadership** goes beyond effective management to **accepting responsibility, being open and honest**, and most of all it is about **caring for the people who work for you**.

Key point:

> Stay in touch without micro-managing. Letting your employees know you are around, that you are interested in them, and that you care, can make all the difference in the world.

[See Dr. Koob's **Work Triology**: *Succeeding at Work*, which includes, *Succeeding with Difficult Coworkers*; *Succeeding with Difficult Bosses*, and *Managing Difficult Employees*]

Difficult Customers

Many businesses are somewhat prepared for customer complaints. Their customer contact people have received extensive training in people skills. Unfortunately, what they often don't provide is **training in understanding the customer: his/her needs, wants, desires, and intent**.

Key point:

Keeping your customers happy has at the root keeping your sales staff and customer service representatives happy, supported, and well-trained.

Revisiting key ideas of communications and interactions with people can be very helpful in maintaining a sales and customer service force that is positive and motivated. These **employees need frequent support and encouragement** as they are often dealing with a good bit of negativity on a regular basis.

It goes without saying that a best business practice is that the "customer is always right." You may lose money on this sale, but if they are satisfied, they will come back, again and again and again.

Difficult family members

The skills in this book work as well with the family as they do in business. It is important to also keep in mind that **caring, love, and affection are paramount needs of human beings**. The family is our primary means of fulfilling these needs. If they are missing or are not being fulfilled, everyone is hurting.

Positivity and the willingness to show and share affection (you may have to be the restarting catalyst) are essential.

Key point with spouses and children: dictatorships don't work. Give everyone a chance to be involved, to have their say.

Questions/ideas for contemplation

Try using some of the skills that have been discussed throughout this book with the significant people in your life. Stay flexible, stay positive.

Remember that the foundation of success can be found in, *The Seven Keys to Understanding and Working with Difficult People.*

Self-Awareness

Self-Worth

Self-Confidence

Self-Control

Honesty

Kindness

Positivity

[See Chapter 13 for a discussion of these Key Ideas.]

Chapter 27

Strangers

Beware, tread lightly

The most important consideration in dealing with strangers is to keep in mind that **you have absolutely no idea** who they are as a person or **what is motivating them**. Without that knowledge, you are not in a position to be totally on top of what is transpiring. **Your most important asset is self-control.**

The techniques we have discussed in this book will very likely be effective; but if you are dealing with a sociopathic person, a drug addict, or someone who is intoxicated, nothing may be effective except avoidance.

When there is any doubt...Safety first!

Get away! Get help! Discretion can be and often IS the better part of valor when dealing with difficult strangers.

It is unfair

You bet it is. When some one is being a bully, treating you or others badly, cutting in line, weaving in and out of traffic dangerously, it is unfair. It is difficult. You are right and they are wrong, and that may be obvious to everyone but the difficult person you are dealing with at this moment in your life.

> Is being RIGHT worth all the angst and fuss you may have to deal with?
>
> Is being right worth having a conflict with someone?
>
> Is being right worth an escalation in the stakes?
>
> Is their rude, obnoxious behavior worth your peace of mind, your life?

Remember, **when you react to their boorish behavior, you are giving up control to them.**

When you maintain control and make more positive chooses,

you gain personal power, you empower yourself.

If you buy into their behavior, you will probably spend far too much of your valuable time being upset, uptight, and unhappy. You are worth more than that. Choose wisely.

Be sure to use tact; kindness; a clear, audible voice tone that is non-threatening, self-control, and patience.

They may be having a difficult day

I could use stronger language here to describe a bad day, but I think you have probably had a few of these yourself and can commiserate. Be compassionate and understanding. You can always say to yourself – been there, done that.

If you have the chance, if you are willing to take that major step back and be a kind and compassionate human being in the face of their less-than-desirable behavior, you could even be the one bright spot in their otherwise miserable day. Stay positive, be positive, if the opportunity presents itself, say something nice to them, or compliment them. It is much better than reacting defensively. You may just be that one person who turns their day around.

Heck, they may be having a difficult life

Difficult people are hurting inside – as we all are when we are being difficult, worrywarts, complaining, blaming, being negative, etc.

Give them the benefit of the doubt. Be positive; stay positive. If the opportunity presents itself, say something nice to them, or compliment them. It is much better than reacting defensively. You may just be the person who helps turn their week, month, year, or even LIFE around.

Dealing with difficult strangers

When you are in a position where you have to deal with a difficult stranger, use the skills you have learned in this book. Use them gently, kindly, positively.

> Get their attention, e.g. "Sir, Sir… Can I help you?"
>
> Help them calm down
>
> Listen attentively and show understanding
>
> Offer to assist if you can

Use humor

This is a skill we haven't discussed yet; it could even be described as an art. Using humor in a difficult situation can be very effective, but it can also be detrimental. You are the only person who can get a feel for the situation well enough to understand if humor might be an appropriate way to get someone to calm down or be something that can help relax the tension of the moment. Use it judiciously.

If you do use humor, don't place the onus on the other person, own it yourself. Make its roots positive.

Questions/ideas for contemplation

Can you imagine using humor effectively in a difficult situation? With a stranger? With your boss, significant other, fellow workers, etc?

Can you envision a scenario where you encounter someone you don't know who is being difficult? How would you respond? What skills and techniques would you use from this book? Be sure to consider, *The Seven Keys to Understanding and Working with Difficult People.*

How do you respond to someone who does something really obnoxious while you are driving – like tailgating, whipping past you, giving you the finger on the way by? How do you feel? How do you deal with those feelings? Do you carry the weight and energy of this encounter with you for hours afterward? Days?

Can you think of a recent situation where you had to deal with someone you didn't know, who was being difficult to you or someone else? How did you deal with it? How would you change your approach now?

Chapter 28

REALLY difficult behaviors

As soon as I start thinking about people who regularly manifest very difficult behaviors, I start thinking of _DIFFICULT_ people. Though my preferred definition for difficult people is virtually all-inclusive of all of humanity, for me, this is where the term actually kicks in.

You may remember the "categories" of difficult people I delineated at the beginning of Part II:

> **Level one**: Most of us; we are occasionally difficult, even though we try our best not to be

> **Level two:** Difficult people who exhibit regular difficult behaviors, though it may not be their intent to be difficult and they may not have any conception that they are difficult.

> If they do know they are difficult, they are often remorseful and feel guilty about their lack of control. Though they may not mean to be, level two difficult people can be very difficult and very hurtful to you and to others.

> **Level three:** _Difficult_ people who know they are difficult and who hurt people on purpose, with no remorse.

Primarily this chapter will be about some specific 'types' of the more difficult of level two difficult people and a bit about level three difficult people.

The hardest people to deal with

People who have strong prejudices and biases can be very difficult to deal with. The techniques and ideas in this book can work with them, but don't be surprised if some people are or seem to be 'beyond help.'

I am reminded of a common movie theme where a key character is incorrigible, prejudiced, etc. but through the course of the movie they 'wake up and smell the roses,' i.e. something happens that helps them to see life in a different way and there is a dramatic change in their approach to others.

Sometimes, in spite of your best efforts and your most positive, compassionate persona, really prejudiced people will not respond. It is always worth your effort to be kind and compassionate with everyone. You may have a positive impact even if it is not obvious. Positivity breeds positivity and we also help ourselves through our own compassionate acts.

129

Sometimes you just have to swallow hard and walk away. In the final analysis, you are responsible for your behavior, not theirs. Be the best person you can be.

Beliefs

Prejudices and biases are based on a certain perspective, a belief system of an individual. Beliefs, no matter how well intentioned, can be a block to flexibility and a block to compassion for others.

This is something worth thinking about because it does affect difficult situations. You can't change another person's belief. You can only bring your own openness and positivity into the mix. Often that will help. Understanding where another person is coming from is helpful to your being able to be successful with them. Work toward understanding who they are and how they look at the world (and you). You will gain wisdom and compassion from this effort.

Phariseeism

Webster defines Pharisaic/Pharisee as: "observing the letter, but not the spirit of religious law," "self-righteous, sanctimonious, hypocritical."

A Pharisaic personality can be very difficult to deal with. **They are very self-righteous** and often see themselves as having the right to force you to believe as they do, or discount you and your life because you don't believe as they do. They think of themselves as better than others and their beliefs are the only **right way** of thinking. They see themselves and those like them as the only true believers.

They are not unique to any particular religion; religious fanatics of any kind fit this category.

They can be very dangerous!

If you have to work with a Pharisaic personality, **avoidance**, as much as possible, is probably the best tactic. Beyond that, be positive, be assertive, be yourself.

Remember that you have the right not to be bullied, put down, or otherwise treated badly. You have the right to stand up for yourself assertively and with as much kindness and compassion you can muster.

The power hungry and greedy

Some people are fanatically driven by a need for power and/or greed. Ultimately, these difficult people should also be avoided. Your skills, self-control, and self-confidence (assertiveness) can be useful in interactions with driven personalities, but don't expect them to change.

True level three difficult people

While you can try the skills and techniques in this book, my advice is if you have the opportunity, **get out.** FAST! If you can't remove yourself from the situation quickly, get help.

Get out, even if it means completely changing your life. This is most likely a no-win situation.

Key point:

> Abusers fit this category. The odds are very, very high that they will abuse again.

Sociopaths, addicts, abusers

These people have serious problems and often cannot control themselves. If you suspect a person to have serious mental problems or you believe they are under the influence of a mind-altering substance, you should back off and, if feasible and/or necessary, report the situation to authorities. They need far more help than you can give them through your interactions with them. They need professional help.

Abusers need professional help, too, and you need to protect yourself and your family.

If they are someone important to you, then try to see that they get help. It is the best thing you can do for them and for yourself. It may be the best thing you can do for others, as well.

If you are working with a person who you feel has serious problems, please contact someone in authority. Most businesses today have forums for reporting serious work-related concerns. Find out what your options are. Human Resources and/or your legal department should have specific information and recommendations about how to proceed. You may also want to consider legal and/or professional aid for yourself. Dealing with a very difficult person can be very stressful and draining.

Make sure that you document in detail any concerns that you have. Keep detailed notes of any incidents, encounters, communications, etc., that you have with this person, or that you witness. Be sure to keep this information private and secure. Keeping it on a work or personal computer is probably not a wise practice.

Sharing information and concerns with a close personal friend or trusted colleague is probably a very good idea. It helps you document your concerns and it is very helpful to have support through stressful situations.

Discretion IS the better part of valor when dealing with very difficult people. **Don't be brave. Be careful and be wise.** You can still be compassionate and kind, because in spite of their serious problems they are 'one of us.'

Luckily, REALLY difficult people are few and far between.

Questions/ideas for contemplation

Knowing your limits is a critical concept in this chapter. Take some moments to think about what your limits are. Be prepared!

Chapter 29

Writing as a tool

Writing can be a very useful tool in working and being successful with difficult people, as well as for helping you work through some of your own stuff with difficult people.

> Author's Note: Some things just seem to make more sense when I write them down. I find it valuable to brainstorm ideas and concerns while typing at the computer or in long hand in a notebook when traveling or waiting for something or someone. Be sure to keep all sensitive materials far from prying eyes. If you choose to keep it; make sure you protect it from access.

Consider adding the skills below to your repertoire of tools that you can use to be successful with the difficult people in your life.

Writing for yourself

Writing down your thoughts and feelings is an excellent way to get and keep a perspective of where you are with the difficult person in your life. The exercises that have been provided at the end of each chapter were designed so that you could take your learning a step further. Going back and revisiting different exercises, writing your ideas and responses, would be an excellent review of information, skills, and personal perspectives that you have learned in this book. [You could think of this as a final exam... Now I'm being difficult!]

It is very helpful to review materials you have worked on several times. Sometimes we come up with our best ideas as we reread and contemplate what we have written before. This practice can also help you gain a perspective of how much you have grown over the weeks and months you have been working with these materials and ideas.

Journaling

Writing down your thoughts and feelings on a daily or weekly basis can give you ongoing insight into concerns, as well as a record of your progress in working with difficult people. You can keep track of your emotions, thoughts, and responses in different difficult situations, and over time see how all of these areas are changing.

It is also amazing how cathartic this can be. You may even find yourself feeling and dealing with some very strong emotions. Be sure to have a support network of close friends available if you feel you need to share your thoughts and feelings. If you feel you are becoming overwhelmed emotionally, you may want to seek professional support and help: counselor, social worker, minister, personal coach, etc.

Challenging yourself to journal on a regular basis can be the best learning tool you have. You should be pleasantly surprised after a length of time to find how you have begun to improve your own attitude, perception and perspective of others, your skills, ability to respond rather than react, and your life in general.

It will also give you the opportunity to see how your developing skills are affecting other people in a positive way.

Writing to clarify

I find it very useful to sit down and write just to clarify things I am thinking about. Often, when we rely only on the thoughts in our head, we start to think in circles; or we can fall into the negative habit of worrying.

Writing can not only help clarify the thinking process, but it also seems to have the effect of keeping our thoughts on track. After all, who wants to write the same thing over and over again?

The written word helps us organize our thoughts, and often helps us begin to develop ideas as well as find solutions that we might not have thought of if we were perseverating about some concern.

Writing to plan

Use writing as a means to delineate and clarify your approach to a difficult person. Planning through a potential interaction with a person can help you think through and detail how you hope to handle yourself. While you cannot predict how the encounter will go, you can develop a repertoire of possible responses; and in the process increase your self-confidence and self-control as you enter the planned meeting.

Be sure to follow through with journaling after your interaction and reflect on what worked, what didn't work, as well as subsequent revisions to your strategy. This is particularly useful to do prior to interacting with a person with whom you have had a history of difficulties.

Writing to work on your feelings

Write to your difficult person. DON'T SEND IT. Write about your frustrations, how you truly feel when they push your buttons, and write down your thoughts. Write until you have gotten all of it out and you start winding down emotionally and mentally.

Then keep writing, if possible, until you can feel a more positive outlook emerging about working with this person. Write as long as you can and get your thoughts out. You might even go right into planning your next positive interaction with them.

Remember DON'T SEND IT! And don't leave it lying around. This is for your personal growth only.

My recommendation: have a little burning ritual (be careful!) Send those bad feelings blowing away in the wind. It can be a cathartic experience. At the very least, put it in a very safe place if you want to revisit it and later return to adding to it.

Writing to feel even better

Writing out affirmations (brief positive statements about yourself) can be very helpful in reminding yourself of what you really want to change from within.

As examples:

"I am good enough"

"I am in-control of Me!"

"I am a positive force in all my interactions with others."

"I am personally powerful."

Turn your negative self-statements around and make them positive, affirming statements. This will help you move from accepting negativity and blame from others, and from constantly kicking yourself, to a more positive approach to life.

Writing affirmations out can be even more powerful.

One technique is to write the same affirmation ten times in several ways. For instance:

"I am good enough." (Repeat nine more times)

"I, Joe, am good enough. (Repeat)

"I am good at my job." (Repeat)

"It is safe for me to be successful." (Repeat)

Another technique is to work with an affirmation and write a brief response after each affirmation:

"I am good enough."

Response: "I don't feel good enough, but I'm working on it."

"I am good enough."

Response: "I would like to feel I am good enough."

"I am good enough."

Response: "I really wish I felt good enough...I'm working on it."

And so on.

Try to keep doing it until you get consistently positive responses. Write whatever pops into your head. Don't think too hard about it. This is from the gut.

Writing for yourself is for you!

Try to think of different ways that you can use writing to facilitate your growth and learning. Write to facilitate and document your progress with difficult people.

Use writing to help your self-work with difficult people.

There are probably thousands of ways that you can integrate writing in continuing your success with difficult people. I will outline a few below, but use your intelligence and imagination. Writing is a great and effective tool used in caring hands.

Keep Records

Keep detailed records. You never know when you might need them and they can help keep you focused on what is important and what you need to do. Keep them safe!

> Author's Note: For the record – I once had an employee get into my office and copy confidential personnel information. Play it safe! Make sure any personal or sensitive information is out of the reach of prying eyes.

Get them to put it in writing!

This is a GREAT tool to use with complainers, blamers, gossipers, backstabbers, and just about any difficult people. Make a firm guideline that you will only listen to their complaints, blaming, etc, if they are presented in a formal memo with one or more solutions attached.

Guess what?

Complainers might just see this as WORK! And the behavior will decrease.

Most difficult people don't want to make this much effort. They might not stop blaming and complaining, but they probably won't do very much of it within your purview.

This also provides you with more documentation. Keep it in a safe place.

Reward written suggestions, especially solution-oriented ideas. In other words, discourage negative behavior and reward positive behavior.

Get passive people to put commitments in writing!

Intermediate steps

If you are working with passive or passive-aggressive types, a useful tool is for them to run drafts of their work by you so you can provide positive feedback and additional encouragement. Be sure they understand that this is for their benefit and they only have to do it if they want to. Give lots of positive feedback along with your advice.

Don't use writing as punishment

Always couch it in terms of positive benefits to the person you are working with. Give them the chance to own what they are doing and suggest their own ideas and processes.

Writing as communication (both ways)

Try to keep in mind everything discussed in this book about using positive communications with difficult people. When you use writing to communicate with a difficult person (e-mails, memos, etc.) keep it positive and keep it terse. Use effective headlines (to draw attention) and almost never write an e-mail or memo longer than a typewritten page. [I always try to keep them at half a page or less.] In today's helter-skelter, 'too busy' work environment, we all tend to table anything that we can't read in a very brief period of time. If you have more to say, attach it or send a separate message at a different time.

Encourage written communications from difficult people. Both of you can learn a good deal from this process. Encourage them to keep you posted on what is important to them and what is important to you.

Always read materials carefully, and when appropriate, respond.

Keep in mind that e-mails and memos tend to feel less personal or personable. You can add a brief personal note to communiqués and/or find ways to be gentle, kind, caring, and compassionate in your written communications. Think about how you might take what you are writing if you received it.

E-mail

Use e-mail memos as a quick and highly effective means of complimenting, encouraging, and praising others. When someone has done well, send the e-mail to the team. This is a great tool for helping to accept someone, especially unresponsive and even belligerent difficult people, into the fold.

Keep them brief – readable at a glance. Then you will be sure people see them.

Positivity breeds positivity! Writing is another tool that you can use to be positive.

Questions/ideas for contemplation

Brainstorm some ideas that could be an effective means of using writing as a tool in dealing with difficult people.

Chapter 30

Wrapping up

Congratulations!

You have reached the final chapter of this book. Now you have significant information and added skills to work with the difficult people in your life. This brief wrap-up will be to reinforce some very key points.

Speaking of reinforcing

The emphasis of a positive approach to understanding and working with difficult people is purposeful – there is already all-together too much negativity in the world.

Here are some additional points in closing.

Losses

Dealing with difficult people can cause us to lose a great deal: our integrity, self-confidence, self-control, feelings of acceptance, peace of mind, and even our health. I hope that one of your goals after completing this book will be to **take care of yourself**. Remember:

When you are not having fun, something is wrong – adjust.

Also, keep in mind that when you take care of yourself, you also are much better able to take care of others.

Respect

Respect difficult people in spite of their difficult people-ism.

Remain in control, be self-confident, be kind and compassionate and many people, even the difficult ones, will come to respect you. They will respect you for who you are and for the effort you are making for them. It may take some time, but it does happen.

Remember about caring

We don't have to be best friends with difficult people. We don't have to socialize with them. But it does pay to care about who they are and what is important to them. They will often come to appreciate it.

Caring goes beyond acceptance.

Remember to learn from difficult people

Whether you believe they were placed in your path for a reason or not, you can learn a tremendous amount from difficult people. It is a positive outlook that you can have that can significantly change your interactions with them. **Attitude IS everything; your attitude!**

Need additional help with your difficult people?

We have trained coaches who work specifically with people who are having problems with difficult people. Take advantage of mini-coaching or coaching to work through specific concerns. Use the links available on our web site: www.difficultpeople.org.

Best wishes

We sincerely hope that this book has been useful. We wish you the utmost success with your difficult situations and the utmost success in life.

Joe Koob

Appendix I

Your true self

I believe that we all have the right to be the best we can be, and part of that process is **accepting that our life's responsibilities rests firmly on our own shoulders**. Through whatever difficulties arise, we have to make the best choices for who we are and who we want to become.

Ask yourself

Who am I and how do I fit into the grand scheme of things?

You can approach this from several perspectives:

Who am I? Deep inside? The real me?

Who do I really want to be?

How am I bringing this conception to reality in this world (at home, at work, with friends)?

Can I bring the inner reality/dream of who I truly want to be to outward fruition?

I believe the best way to get at who you are fundamentally as a human being, the true you, as it were, is to do a little exercise I developed for my book *Guiding Children*.

Who we are fundamentally is based on what we really value. If we consider the qualities that we would want our children to have and develop as they grow up, I believe we are touching the basis for what we truly value in ourselves. Try this exercise:

What ten qualities or values would you like to instill in your children as they grow? Make a list.

Try to be specific and to keep the number at or below ten fundamental qualities. Stick with values and qualities, i.e. don't put in things like, "I want Marsha to be a surgeon."

When you have a solid list, start to prioritize. Pick the top five values you would like them to have; then narrow it to three. See if you can get it down to the one most important, fundamental quality you would like your child to have. Then put the list back together in order of priority.

Chances are this list describes what your ideal of YOU is.

141

Need help getting started? At the end of this section is a list of 99 values/qualities I used for my book, *Honoring Work and Life: 99 Words for Leaders to Live By*.

This list is by no means exhaustive. Find the best words that work for your vision.

After you have developed your list, print it out and carry it with you; or post it in a place where you will encounter it frequently. You can also make a small-print version, laminate it, and carry it in your wallet or purse.

Another Perspective

Another means of understanding what you truly value is to ask your self these questions:

> How would you like your life to be remembered?

> What would you like engraved on your tombstone – the final comment on who you were?

These are very personal considerations and you may find thinking about them a bit difficult; but when we are willing to make the effort, it does help us **focus on what is most important**. If you feel it could help, you could discuss this approach with a close friend or relative. When we consider these types of questions, it places our whole life in perspective; and it can give us a fundamental ideal or concept to continually strive for.

Here's the clincher

In every interaction you have,

> How are you manifesting the qualities of your ideal you?

> How do you bring what you value most to the fore?

> How many moments of your existence from this point on can you live fulfilling this personal image?

The more you can be you, the you of your deepest values and qualities, the easier your relationships with difficult others will be… and the more joyous and fulfilling your life will be, too.

1. Integrity
2. Honesty**
3. Trust
4. Ownership
5. Accountable
6. Responsibility
7. Reliability
8. Self-control**
9. Loyalty
10. Committed
11. Conscientious
12. Credible
13. Stability
14. Continuity
15. Disciplined
16. Humility
17. Idealism
18. Service
19. Appreciation
20. Acknowledgment
21. Respect
22. Courteous
23. Attention
24. Support
25. Grateful
26. Recognition
27. Celebration

28. Ceremony

29. Reward

30. Caring

31. Kindness**

32. Empathy

33. Compassion

34. Patience

35. Generous

36. Responsiveness

37. Grace

38. Self-awareness**

39. Awareness

40. Visibility

41. Connecting

42. Modeling

43. Self-worth**

44. Self-respect

45. Self-confidence**

46. Character

47. Identity

48. Quality

49. Value-added

50. Stretching

51. Learning

52. Education

53. Renewal

54. Solution-focused

55. Catalyst

56. Cultivate

57. Rigorous

58. Persistence

59. Synthesizer

60. Cohesion

61. Attitude

62. Consistent

63. Cooperative

64. Competent

65. Discerning

66. Focus

67. Organized

68. Engagement

69. Determined

70. Energy

71. Down-to-earth

72. Simplicity

73. Creativity

74. Innovation

75. Flexibility

76. Experiment

77. Risk-taking

78. Fluidity

79. Chances

80. Imagination

81. Friction-free

82. Anticipates

83. Facilitates

84. Curiosity

85. Initiative

86. Choices

87. Passion

88. Vision

89. Conviction

90. Courage

91. Fearless

92. Zany

93. Spontaneous

94. Zesty

95. Intensity

96. Charisma

97. Showmanship

98. Positivity**

99. Symbolizes

**The Seven Keys to Understanding and Working with Difficult People

CHOICES

I am going to worry all the time and kick myself
whenever I do something
that is remotely stupid.

I am going to feel bad whenever anyone puts me
down, be depressed because no one likes me,
and get frustrated all the time
because no one listens to me.

I am not going to take care of myself when I get
tired, over-worked, or ill
or take time for myself because I have way too
much to do.

I am going to accept everything bad that anyone
says about me,
because it's all true.

I am going to wallow in self-pity.

Or

*I am going to stop worrying and look at the
brighter side of life.*

*I am going to pay attention to my thoughts
and feelings and when I start to think negatively
or to kick myself,*

*I am going to turn my thoughts around and say
supportive, kind things to myself.*

*I am going to be self-confident, believe in myself,
and maintain a calm, cool, collected persona
wherever I am and with whomever I am with.*

*I am going to be assertive, kind, and compassionate
in all my dealings with others.*

*I am going to pay attention to my communications
and always try to present
a positive me to the rest of the world.*

I am going to believe in myself.
difficultpeople.org

Bibliographies

Bibliography of Dr. Koob's Books

Annotated Bibliography

Understanding and Working with Difficult People

We believe this book presents the most comprehensive material available about being successful with difficult people. This book is designed to be a practical, accessible introduction to the very broad topic of dealing with difficult people/difficult behaviors. Since every difficult situation is different, the focus here will be on building a basic understanding of how you interact with difficult people, what makes difficult people tick, and the most fundamental skills you can bring to the table to help change these encounters for the better.

ME! A Difficult Person?

This is second of our signature books. This book focuses on learning more about yourself. Most of us are occasionally difficult or seen as difficult by others. This may simply be a matter of different perspectives, or it may mean that we have some inner work to do. This course is concerned with understanding more about how you come across to others, and understanding more about who you are as a person. It is also concerned with self-improvement – making changes that will help make your interactions with others significantly better, and that will bring you more peace, comfort, and joy in your life.

Difficult Spouses? Improving and Saving Your Relationship with Your Significant Other

Are you having difficulties in your current relationship? Facing a divorce? Newly divorced and trying to understand what happened and what you could have done about it? We feel this book has value not only for couples who are simply having difficulties in their relationships with their significant others, but also those facing divorce, recently divorced couples, and for people entering new relationships. The focus is on developing the knowledge, skills, and tools to help your relationship be successful.

Dealing with Difficult Strangers

Being successful in difficult situations with strangers is all about what you can bring to the situation. You will find a tremendous amount of useful information and skills included in this book that can make a significant difference in how you approach difficult strangers, how you feel as a result of these difficult encounters, and how you can emerge without a negative experience having ruined your day.

Succeeding with Difficult Professors (and Tough Courses)

A course for college students at all levels. What you need to know to make the most of your college career. This course has two main sections: "Getting along with Difficult Professors," and "Succeeding in Tough Classes." The first section will discuss ideas and skills you can use to get through personal difficulties with professors. The second section will focus on techniques, study skills, and approaches that will help you get the grades you want.

Guiding Children

Guiding and working with children is on the mind of every parent. This book focuses on skills and tools to help you as a parent provide the best possible environment for your child's development by avoiding difficulties through intelligent upbringing. This book is not only about helping you to guide your children through concerns that arise, but it is even more about enjoying your children. They do grow up, much faster than we expect. Take advantage of the tremendous joy they can bring into your life and the vast understanding of life that they provide. You will be glad you did.

Dealing with Difficult Customers

(for Employees, Companies, and Customer Service Personnel)

This book is all about putting the gamut of customer relations and interactions into a perspective that is workable, livable, and supports you, the customer contact person, throughout.

While many businesses do provide extensive customer relations training, the focus is often fairly one way – aimed at keeping business. We present you with extensive insight and knowledge about the customer's perspective, what you need to know as a company representative to fulfill your job, the internal and external support you need, and the tools and skills to communicate effectively with difficult customers.

Caring for Difficult Patients: A Guide for Nursing Professionals

I believe that the Nursing profession is one of the most admired in America. We think of Nurses as professional: that is, they have a knowledge base and skill set that is unique and valued – the quality of their work is important to them; and we think of Nurses as people who care about their patients – they are concerned with our well-being when we are under their care. These considerations are the focal point for discussing how to best deal with difficult patients.

Trilogy: Dealing with Change

Books centered on Leaders working through change:

Difficult Situations - Dealing with Change

Change and difficult situations can certainly produce a great deal of angst, and as a result, difficult people. This book focuses on learning the skills and tools you need to deal with the ongoing stresses of constant change in the business world today. It is about knowledgeable leadership: how what you do helps you get through change, and more importantly helps you lead others through change. It presumes you are already inspired, good, intelligent, and practical. This book is about making a difference.

Honoring Work and Life: 99 Words for Leaders to Live By

This book provides a foundation of key ideas that focus on Leadership and Personal qualities, attributes, and behaviors that honor not only our work but our life. It is my firm belief that true leaders work to serve their fellow employees, their team, their company, their customers, as well as their families and friends. This is about understanding and working on those attributes that make great leaders.

Leaders Managing Change

Leaders Managing Change is about understanding and dealing with the ongoing stresses of constant change in the business world today, but most importantly it is about leadership. When I thought about the concerns that are a regular part of high turnover rates, leadership changes, acquisitions and mergers, and the myriad of other transitions businesses face today, the focus came down to leadership. Good leaders get things done. This book focuses on knowledgeable leadership (i.e. what you need to know to help you deal with change as a leader). It presumes you are already inspired, good, intelligent, and practical. This book is about making a difference.

Business Trilogy

Dealing with Difficult Coworkers

The emphasis here is on helping people solve the difficulties they have at work with someone who is relatively speaking a 'coworker,' or 'colleague,' in other words, someone whose 'rank' or 'job' is roughly on the same level as yours. Are you perturbed, exasperated, frustrated, angry, upset, and genuinely peeved with someone at work? We have all had occasion to work with someone who seems to have a wide range of concerns with other people in the workplace. Can we succeed with them and turn a difficult situation around? Can we enjoy our work-life once again? Definitely! This book provides you with key ideas, skills, and tools that you can use to be successful with difficult colleagues. The power is in your own inner strength and the knowledge and understanding you develop.

Succeeding with Difficult Bosses

Have a tough boss? This is a practical, in-the-trenches approach to succeeding with a difficult authority figure – a (how to) book for one of your most important relationships at work. This book is specifically focused on understanding the unique relationship we have with a person who has hierarchical power over us. To truly gain the knowledge we need to be successful with difficult bosses, we need to understand who they are as a person and what they do that frustrates us. We must also understand ourselves – how we subconsciously add to the mix, and how we can change our outlook and behavior so that our boss will change his/her behavior in relationship to us. When people talk about 'difficult' bosses, the root of their concerns is often that they FEEL left out, unappreciated, put down, 'less than,' i.e., treated almost as a non-entity. If you feel this way, this book was written for you

Managing Difficult Employees

This book is about what YOU as a manager and leader bring to the table. It addresses two key questions: Is your leadership conducive to a positive work environment with few personnel concerns; and, when concerns do arise, are you prepared to handle them effectively and efficiently? The first part of this book focuses on avoiding difficulties through knowledgeable and inspired leadership. Part II of this work will demonstrate how to apply your personal strengths and your management and leadership skills to working successfully with difficult personnel concerns and in difficult situations.

A Perfect Day: Guide for a Better Life
Dr. Koob's award-winning book about working toward your own personal perfect day – Best Book Non-fiction, 1999, Oklahoma Writer's Federation; Writer's Digest Merit Award 2000. [Available at on-line retailers]

Difficult People Materials

Axelrod, A and Holtje, J., *201 Ways to Deal with Difficult People*, McGraw-Hill, New York, 1997.

Bell, A. and Smith, D., *Winning with Difficult People*, Barron's, New York, 1997

Bramson, Robert M., *Coping with Difficult Bosses*, Fireside, New York, 1992.

Bramson, Robert M., *Coping with Difficult People*, Anchor Press, New York, 1981.

Braunstein, Barbara, *How to Deal with Difficult People*, Skillpath Publications, Mission, KS, 1994. [Tapes]

Brinkman, R. and Kirschner, R., *Dealing with People You Can't Stand,* McGraw-Hill, New York, 1994.

Carter, Jay, *Nasty Bosses: How to STOP BEING HURT by them without stooping to THEIR level*, McGraw-Hill, New York, 2004.

Case, Gary and Rhoades-Baum, *How to Handle Difficult Customers*, Help Deck Institute, Colorado Springs, 1994.

Cava, Roberta, *Dealing with Difficult People: How to Deal with Nasty Customers, Demanding Bosses and Annoying Co-workers*, Firefly Books, Buffalo, NY, 2004.

Cava, Roberta, *difficult people: How to Deal with Impossible clients, Bosses, and Employees*, Firefly Books, Buffalo, NY, 1990.

Cavaiola, A. And Lavender, N., *Toxic Coworkers: How to Deal with Dysfunctional People on the Job*, New Harbinger Publications, Oakland, CA, 2000.

Costello, Andrew, *How to Deal with Difficult People*, Ligori Publications, Liguri, MI, 1980.

Crowe, Sandra, *Since Strangling Isn't An Option*, Perigee, New York, 1999.

Diehm, William, *How to Get Along with Difficult People*, Broadman Press, Nashville, 1992.

Felder, Leonard, *Does Someone Treat You Badly? How to Handle Brutal Bosses, Crazy Coworkers...and Anyone Else Who Drives You Nuts*, Berkley Books, NY, 1993.

First, Michael, Ed., *Diagnostic and Statistical Manual for Mental Disorders*, 4th Edition, American Psychiatric Asso.,Washington, 1994.

Friedman, Paul, *How to Deal with Difficult People*, SkillPath Publications, Mission, KS, 1994.

Gill, Lucy, *How to Work with Just About Anyone*, Fireside, New York, 1999.

Griswold, Bob, *Coping with Difficult and Negative People and Personal Magnetism*, Effective Learning Systems, Inc., Edina, MN. [Tape]

Holloway, Andy, "Bad Boss Blues," *Canadian Business*, 24 Oct 2004.

Hoover, John, *How to Work for an Idiot: Survive & Thrive Without Killing Your Boss*, Career Press, Princeton, NJ, 2004.

Jones, Katina, *Succeeding with Difficult People*, Longmeadow Press, Stamford, CT, 1992.

Keating, Charles, *Dealing with Difficult People*, Paulist Press, New York, 1984.

Littauer, Florence, *How to Get Along with Difficult People*, Harvest House, Eugene, 1984.

Lloyd, Ken, *Jerks at Work: How to Deal with People Problems and Problem People*, Career Press, Franklin Lakes, NJ, 1999

Lundin, W. and Lundin, J., *When Smart People Work for Dumb Bosses: How to Survive in a Crazy and Dysfunctional Workplace*, McGraw-Hill, New York, 1998.

Markham, Ursula, *How to deal with Difficult people*, Thorsons, London, 1993.

Meier, Paul, *Don't Let Jerks Get the Best of You: Advice for Dealing with Difficult People*, Thomas Nelson, Nashville, 1993.

Namie, G. and Namie, R., *the Bully at Work*, Sourcebooks, Inc., Naperville, IL, 2000.

Osbourne, Christina, *Dealing with Difficult People*, DK, London, 2002.

Oxman, Murray, *The How to Easily Handle Difficult People, Success Without Stress*, Morro Bay, CA, 1997.

Perkins, Betty, *Lion Taming: The Courage to Deal with Difficult People Including Yourself*, Tzedakah Publications, Scramento, 1995.

Rosen, Mark, *Thank You for Being Such A Pain: Spiritual Guidance for Dealing with Difficult People*, Three Rivers Press, New York, 1998.

Segal, Judith, *Getting Them to See It Your Way: Dealing with Difficult and Challenging People*, Lowell House, Los Angeles, 2000.

Solomon, Muriel, *Working with Difficult People*, Prentice Hall, Englewood Cliffs,1990.

Toropov, Brandon, *The Complete Idiot's Guide to Getting Along with Difficult People*, Alpha Books, New York, 1997.

Toropov, Brandon, *Manager's Guide to Dealing with Difficult People*, Prentice Hall, Paramus, NJ, 1997.

Turecki, Stanley, *The Difficult Child*, Bantam Books, NY, 1989.

Weiner, David L., *Power Freaks: Dealing with Them in the Workplace or Anywhere*, Prometheus Books, Amherst, New York, 2002

Weiss, Donald, *How to Deal with Difficult People*, Amacon, New York, 1987.

Recommended Readings

Dewey, John, *Democracy and Education*, Norwood Press, Norwood, MA, 1916.

Dewey, John, *Education and Experience*, Kappa Delta Pi Publications, Macmillian, New York, 1938.

Dyer, Wayne, *Pulling Your Own Strings*, Funk and Wagnalls, New York, 1978.

Dyer, Wayne, *Your Erroneous Zones*, Funk and Wagnalls, New York, 1976.

Dyer, Wayne, *Your Sacred Self*, Harper, New York, 1995.

Guraik, David B., Editor, *Webster's New World Dictionary*, World Publishing, New York, 1972.

Heinlein, Robert, *Time Enough for Love*, New English Library, New York, 1974.

Hesse, Hermann, *Narcissus and Goldmund*, Bantam, New York, 1971.

James, M, and Jongeward, D. *Born to Win*, Addison-Wesley, 1971.

Koob, Joseph, *A Perfect Day: Guide for A Better Life*, NEJS Publications, Lawton, OK, 1998.

Parrott, Thomas Marc, Ed., *Shakespeare: Twenty-three Plays and the Sonnets*, Charles Scribner's Sons, Washington, D.C., 1938.

Pirsig, Robert, *Zen and the Art of Motorcycle Maintenance*, Bantam, New York, 1980.

Rand, Ayn, *Atlas Shrugged*, Signet Books, New York, 1957.

Redman, Ben Ray, Editor, *The Portable Voltaire*, Viking Press, New York, 1949.

Change and Leadership

Bolles, Richard N., *What Color is Your Parachute?* Ten Speed Press, Berkeley, CA, 1987.

Bridges, William, *Managing Transitions: Making the Most of Change*, Perseus Books, Cambridge, 1991.

Bridges, William, *Transitions: Making Sense of Life's Changes*, Perseus Books, Cambridge, 1980.

Buckingham, Marcus, & Coffman, Curt, *First, Break All the Rules: What the World's Greatest Managers Do Differently*, Simon and Schuster, New York, 1999.

Collins, J., and Porras, J., *Built to Last: Successful Habits of Visionary Companies*, Harper Business, NY, 2001.

Collins, Jim, *Good TO Great: Why Some Companies Make the Leap...and Others Don't*, Harper Business, NY, 2001.

Cooper, Robert and Sawaf, Ayman, *Executive EQ: Emotional Intelligence in Leadership & Organizations*, Grisset/Putnam, New York, 1996.

Crane, Thomas, *The Heart of Coaching*, FTA Press, San Diego, 1998.

Deits, Bob, Life *After Loss: A Personal Guide Dealing with Death, Divorce, Job Change and Relocation*, Fisher Books, Tucson, 1988.

Dominhguez, Linda R., *How to Shine at Work*, McGraw Hill, 2003.

Drucker, Peter F., *Managing in a Time of Great Change*, Truman Talley Books, NY, 1995.

Evard, Beth L. And Gipple, Craig A., *Managing Business Change for Dummies*, Hungry Minds, Inc., NY,2001.

Farson, Richard and Keyes, Ralph, *Whoever Makes the Most Mistakes Wins: The Paradox of Innovation*, Free Press, NY, 2002.

Fortgang, Laura Berman, *Take Yourself to the Top: The Secrets of America's #1 Career Coach*, Warner Books, New York, 1998.

Gates, Bill, *Business @ the Speed of Thought: Succeeding in the Digital Economy*, Warner Books, New York, 1999.

Gerstner, Jr., Louis, V, *Who Says Elephants Can't Dance? Leading a Great Enterprise Through Dramatic Change*, HarperBusiness, New York, 2002.

Going Through Bereavement–When a loved one dies, Langeland Memorial Chapel, Kalamazoo, MI.

Grieve, Bradly T., *The Blue Day Book: A Lesson in Cheering Yourself Up*, Andrews McMeel Publishing, Kansas City, 2000.

Goldratt, Eliyahu M., *Critical Chain*, North River Press, Great Barrington, MA, 1997.

Hammer, Michael and Champy, James, *Reengineering the Corporation: A Manifesto for Business Revolution, HarperBusiness*, New York, 1993.

Hoffer, Eric, *The Ordeal of Change*, Harper & Row, NY, 1952.

Jeffreys, J. Shep. *Coping with Workplace Change: Dealing with Loss and Grief*, Crisp Productions, Menlo Park, CA, 1995.

Johnson, Spencer, *Who Moved My Cheese*, G. P. Putnam, New York, 1998.

Kanter, Rosabeth Moss, *The Change Masters: Innovation & Entrepreneurship in the American Corporation*, Simon & Schuster, New York, 1983.

Kelley, Robert, *How to be a Star at Work: Nine Breakthrough Strategies You Need to Succeed*, Random House, New York, 1998.

Koob, Joseph E. II, *Difficult Situations: Dealing with Change*, NEJS Publications, Saline, MI, 2004.

Kotter, John P, *Leading Change*, Harvard Business School Press, Boston, 1996.

Kotter, John P, *The Leadership Factor*, Free Press, New York, 1988.

Kouzes, J. and Posner, B., *Credibility: How Leaders Gain and Lose it; Why People Demand it*, Jossey-Bass Publishers, San Francisco, 1993.

Kuster, Elizabeth, *Exorcising Your Ex*, Fireside, New York, 1996.

Leonard, George, *Mastery: The Keys to Success and Long-term Fulfillment*, Plume, NY 1992.

Lunden, Joan, and Cagan, Andrea, *A Bend in the Road is Not the End of the Road,* William Morrow, New York, 1998.

Maxwell, John C., *The 21 Indispensible Qualities of Leadership: Becoming the Person Others Will Want to Follow*, Thomas Nelson Publishers, Nashville, 1999.

Maxwell, John C., *The 17 Indisputable Laws of Teamwork: Embrace them and Empower Your Team*, Thomas Nelson Publishers, Nashville, 2001.

Maxwell, John C., *21 Irrefutable Laws of Leadership*, Thomas Nelson, Inc., Nashville, 1998.

Milwid, Beth, *Working With Men: Professional Women Talk About Power, Sexuality, and Ethics*, Beyond Words, Kingsport, TN, 1990.

McKay, Harvey, *Swim with the Sharks: Without Being Eaten Alive*, William Morrow Co., New York, 1988.

Messer, Bonnie J., *Dealing with Change*, Abington Press, 1996.

Montalbo, Thomas, *The Power of Eloquence: Magic Key to Success in Public Speaking*, Prentive-Hall, Englewood Cliffs, N.J., 1984.

Pasternack, Bruce and Viscio, Albert, *The Centerless Corporation: A New Model for Transforming Your Organization for Growth and Prosperity*, Fireside, New York, 1998.

Peters, Tom, *The Circle of Innovation: You Can't Shrink Your Way to Greatnness*, Vintage Books, New York, 1999.

Peters, Tom, *Liberation Management: Necessary Disorganization for the Nanosecond Nineties*, Faucett Columbine, New York, 1992.

Peters, Tom, and Waterman, Robert, *In Search of Excellence: Lessons from America's Best-Run Companies*, Harper & Row, New York, 1982.

Peters, Tom, and Austin, Nancy, *A Passion for Excellence: The Leadership Difference*, Random House, New York, 1985.

Peters, Tom, *The Pursuit of WOW! Every Person's Guide to Topsy-Turvy Times*, Vintage Books, New York, 1994.

Peters, Tom, *Professional Service Firm 50: Fifty Ways to Transform Your "Department" into a Professional Service Firm whose Trademarks are Passion and Excellence*, Alfred A. Knopf, 1999.

Peters, Tom, *Re-imagine! Business Excellence in a Disruptive Age*, DK, London, 2003.

Peters, Tom, *Thriving on Chaos: Handbook for a Management Revolution*, Alfred Knopf, New York, 1987

Popcorn, Faith, *EVEolutuon: The Eight Truths of Marketing to Women*, Hyperion Books, 2001.

Smith, Hyrum W. The *10 Natural Laws of Successful Time and Life Management: Proven Strategies for Increased Productivity and Inner Peace*, Warner Books, New York, 1994.

Talbot, Kay, *The Ten Biggest Myths About Grief*, Abbey Press, St. Meinrad, IN, 2000.

Waterman, Robert H., Jr., *The Renewal Factor: How The Best Get And Keep The Competitive Edge*, Bantam, New York, 1986.

Whitmore, John, *Coaching for Performance*, Nicholas Brealey Publishing, London, 1999.